THE

SPANISH PASTORAL ROMANCES

BY

HUGO A. RENNERT, Ph.D. (Freiburg i. B.)

BIBLO and TANNEN
NEW YORK
1968

Originally published 1912

Reprinted, 1968, by arrangement with
The University of Pennsylvania Press

by

Biblo and Tannen Booksellers and Publishers, Inc.
63 Fourth Avenue   New York, N.Y. 10003

Library of Congress Catalog Card No. 67-29552

Printed in U.S.A. by
NOBLE OFFSET PRINTERS, INC.
NEW YORK 3, N. Y.

TO THE MEMORY OF

MY MOTHER

MAY 19, 1835—JUNE 5, 1899

PREFACE.

THE first edition of this work was accepted by the faculty of the University of Freiburg i. B. as a dissertation for the degree of Doctor of Philosophy in 1891, and was published in Baltimore in the following year. In its day it was not unfavorably received, and as it has long since been out of print, it has seemed that a new edition might not be unwelcome.

In the long period that has intervened the Pastoral Romance never entirely lost for me its old attraction, and as I gradually acquired many of the early editions of these works and re-read them, I determined to re-issue these "primicias de mi corto ingenio," adding such new facts as subsequent researches had brought to light. The result is the present work, which has been almost entirely rewritten, and now appears, as I hope, in a much improved form. I have not seen fit to change, in any material degree, the opinions originally expressed concerning the various romances; repeated reading has convinced me more than ever that the *Diana* of Montemayor, which was the first, is also the best of these pastorals, while it has increased my admiration for the poetical portions of the *Arcadia* of Lope de Vega.

The Pastoral Romance was essayed by some of the greatest *ingenios* that Spain has produced, and while many of these poets "had no true vocation for the business," as Professor Fitzmaurice-Kelly says of Cervantes, and, as a consequence, their works are of widely varying degrees of merit, yet they cannot be entirely neglected by the student, for the pastoral is a product of the most flourishing period of Spanish literature,—a literature unsurpassed by any in the modern world.

H. A. R.

TABLE OF CONTENTS.

THE

SPANISH PASTORAL ROMANCES

INTRODUCTION

THE appearance of the pastoral romance in Spain in
the middle of the sixteenth century, and the extreme favor
with which it was received, may, in view of the social condition of the country, seem at first sight paradoxical. At
the time of the accession of Philip the Second, Spain was
at the zenith of her military greatness. Her possessions
were scattered from the North Sea to the islands of the
Pacific, and her conquests had been extended over both
parts of the western world.[1] The constant wars against
the Moors, and the stirring ballads founded upon them,
had fostered an adventurous and chivalric spirit,—a dis-
tinguishing trait of the Spanish character. Arms and the
church were the only careers that offered any opportunity
for distinction, and every Spanish gentleman was, first of
all, a soldier.

Such a state of society was favorable for books of chivalry, which, beginning with *Amadis de Gaula,* made their
appearance at the beginning of the sixteenth century,[2] and

---

[1] The Spanish language was, for the greater part of Europe, the
chief medium of communication between nations. See Cervantes,
Persiles y Sigismunda, Vol. II, Book iii.

[2] The whole subject of *Amadis* has been reviewed in his masterly
way by D. Marcelino Menéndez Y Pelayo, *Orígenes de la Novela,* Mad-

9

soon enjoyed a popularity that was unparalleled. For half a century these *Libros de Caballerías* held undisputed sway. Gradually, however, the readers, especially those in court circles, grew weary of the monotonous and impossible exploits of the paladins, and their desire for a change was soon gratified. How these books of chivalry, in the beginning of the following century, " were smiled away from out the world " by *Don Quixote,* we have often been told.[1] But nearly fifty years before the appearance of the

rid, 1905, Vol. I. The conclusions at which the distinguished critic arrives are briefly: That *Amadis* is a very free imitation of the breton cycle; that it existed prior to 1325; that the author of the rescension made in the time of King Denis was probably Juan Lobeira, *miles,* of whom we possess poems written between 1258 and 1286; that the cancion of *Leonoreta* inserted in the present version of *Amadis* is certainly his; that we have not sufficient data to affirm in what language the primitive *Amadis* was written; that it was known in Castile since the time of Chancellor Ayala, and is mentioned by Pero Ferrús in the *Cancionero de Baena;* that the traditions concerning Vasco de Lobeira, preserved by Azurara, is worthy of little credit, and that the only literary form in which we possess the *Amadis* is the Spanish text of Garci Ordoñez de Montalvo, of which the edition of 1508 is the earliest known, and which was certainly not finished till after 1492. *Ibid.,* pp. ccxxii ff. It may be added that Prof. Baist still maintains that *Amadis* is of Spanish origin (Gröber's *Grundriss,* Vol. II, 2 Abt., pp. 416, 438-441.

According to Foulché-Delbosc the earliest mention of *Amadis,* in which the name is coupled with *Tristan* and *Cifar,* is found in a book written before 1350, (and perhaps before 1345), and published in 1494, entitled *Regimento de los Príncipes,* printed at Seville by Meynardo Ungut and Stanislao Polono. It is a translation of the *De Regimine Principum* of Egidio Colonna, made by Johan Garcia de Castrogeriz. *Revue Hispanique* (1906), p. 815. The only known copy of *Amadis* of the edition of Çaragoça, 1508, is now in the British Museum. The question of *Amadis* is once more reviewed by G. E. Williams, in the *Revue Hispanique,* Vol. XXI (1909).

[1] The truth is, that by the beginning of the seventeenth century the romances of chivalry were about at their last gasp. As Fitzmaurice-Kelly says: " They continued, though in diminishing numbers, and so late as 1602 Juan de Silva y de Toledo published his *Historia famosa*

Knight of La Mancha, a new form of fiction appeared in Spain,[1] which soon gained the ascendency over its older rival. This was the Pastoral Romance.

The pastoral romance was, in a measure, an offspring of the romance of chivalry. Its beginnings are already clearly discernible in some of the followers of *Amadis*. In the *Libro noveno de Amadís, que es la Chronica del muy valiente y esforzado Principe y Cavallero de la Ardiente Espada, Amadis de Grecia, hijo de Lisuarte de Grecia*, of which an edition printed at Burgos, 1553, is cited by Gayangos, the pastoral element is already introduced. Darinel and Sylvia, shepherd and shepherdess, are brought upon the scene and play an important part in the books that follow. As Gayangos says: " The pastoral romance, cultivated since the beginning of the century by Sannazaro and the Italians, now began to be known in Spain, and was afterwards carried to the highest degree of perfection by Montemayor.[2] In *Don Florisel de Niquea*, the first two

---

del *Príncipe don Policisne de Beocia.* Don Policisne de Beocia was the last of his race. Cervantes's book appeared three years later. It did instantly what sermons and legislation had failed to do. After the publication of *Don Quixote* no new chivalresque romance was issued, and of ancient favourites only Diego Ortúñez de Calahorra's *Caballero del Febo* was reprinted (1617-23). The fictitious knights were slowly dying; Cervantes slew them at a blow." *Don Quixote*, translated by John Ormsby, edited by Jas. Fitzmaurice-Kelly, Glasgow, 1901, Vol. I, p. xxii.

[1] The long line of picaresque novels also began at this time, *Lazarillo de Tormes* appearing in 1553(?).

[2] *Libros de Caballerias, con un Discurso preliminar y un Catálogo razonado*, por Don Pascual de Gayangos. Madrid, Ribadeneyra, 1857, p. xxxi. It is not within the scope of this work to trace the beginnings of pastoral poetry in Spain. Nearly twenty years before the appearance of Montemayor's *Diana*, the influence of the Italian pastorals is clear in the works of Garcilaso de la Vega, whose " Eclogues " first appeared in 1543, with the works of Boscan, another poet entirely under the influence of the Italians. That Garcilaso was an imi-

parts of which appeared at Valladolid in 1532, we already see Don Florisel assuming the garb of a shepherd and following the shepherdess Sylvia, with whom he had fallen in love. And in the fourth part of *Don Florisel de Niquea,* of which there is an edition dated Salamanca, 1551, *romances, quintillas* and eclogues, which the author calls *bucólicos,* are introduced into romances of chivalry for the first time, while the second book of the fourth part of *Don Florisel* (chap. xxxvii), contains an eclogue between two shepherds, Archileo and Laris, and a number of *certámenes* or poetical contests, in the manner of those which Montemayor afterwards introduced into his *Diana.*[1]

The marked favor with which the Spanish pastoral romance was greeted, and the signal success it immediately enjoyed, may, perhaps, be explained (in addition to the reason already given) by the fact that the *Diana,* its first representative, was a work of real genius, while the peculiar temperament and susceptibility of the Spanish people were, doubtless, also a factor in its success. But, as already stated, the pastoral romance was not originally a growth of the Spanish soil, but was transplanted from Italy, its home.

Spain and Italy had long been in close communication; Sicily had been subject to the crown of Aragon since 1282; Milan and the Kingdom of Naples had come into the possession of Spain, and Spanish troops under Charles V. had overrun the whole Italian peninsula. Such continued con-

tator of Sannazaro, going at times even to the extent (as in his second Eclogue) of translating almost verbally whole passages of the *Arcadia,* has been shown by Torraca, *Gl'Imitatori Stranieri di Jacopo Sannazaro,* Roma, 1882. All that has been written heretofore upon the origins of the pastoral in Spain has now been superseded by the work of Menéndez y Pelayo, *Orígenes de la Novela,* Madrid, 1905. Vol. I.

[1] Gayangos, *Libros de Caballerias,* p. xxxvi.

tact with Italy, then the most cultured and refined nation of Europe, could not fail to influence the minds of its invaders; their intellectual horizon was widened, and their thoughts diverted into new channels. There, in the afterglow of the great revival of learning, they found new poetic forms—strangers to their literature, and henceforth the pastoral, amongst other Italian measures, was destined to find a home beyond the Pyrenees.[1]

It was the *Ameto* of Boccaccio, a pastoral in prose and verse, that served, in Italy, as a model for the later pastorals of Sannazaro and Bembo, and for the dramatic pastorals of Tasso and Guarini. Though not strictly a pastoral romance, it prepared the way for this kind of composition, and under its influence Sannazaro, a Neapolitan, born in 1458, wrote his *Arcadia,* which he first published in 1504.[2] Though Sannazaro took the *Ameto* for his model,—which is manifest in the distorted and artificial style which sometimes disfigures the otherwise graceful narrative of the *Arcadia,*—the ancient writers were not without influence in the composition of the latter work. Indeed, Scherillo says that the true master of Sannazaro

[1] The influence of Italy upon the Spanish poet was immense, and includes, almost without exception, every great name from the Marquis of Santillona to Lope de Vega. The earliest and best of the Spanish anthologies, the *Flores de Poetas ilustres* of Pedro de Espinosa, Valladolid, 1605, clearly shows how wide was the influence of Italy. Here we find imitations of Petrarch, Sannazaro, Ariosto, Bernardo and Torquato Tasso, Pánfilo Sasso, Luigi Groto, Girolamo Parabosco, and others.

[2] A mutilated edition of the *Arcadia* appeared at Venice in 1502, but it was without the author's knowledge or consent, and while he was absent in France. See Michele Scherillo, *La Arcadia di Jacopo Sannazaro secondo i Manoscritti e le prime Stampe,* con note ed introduzione. Torino, 1888, in which the *Arcadia* and its sources are discussed with a thoroughness that leaves little to be said. Upon the influence of the Italian pastoral in Spain, see Menéndez y Pelayo, *Orígines de la Novela,* Vol. I, Mad., 1905.

was Virgil.[1] But further [2] on he remarks: " If the Greek and Latin writers provided Sannazaro with the pastoral material, the *form* of the romance was furnished by that one of the three great Tuscans who had come to preach in Naples " la buona novella della nuova lingua," that is, Boccaccio. And again: " the whole fabric of the *Arcadia* is woven upon that of the *Ameto*." [3]

The *Arcadia* is a series of twelve eclogues in verse, interspersed with prose that was written afterward, merely to provide a background and to join them together: but the mixed form of prose and verse, given to this species of composition, and which was already present in the *Ameto*, was ever afterward retained by all the Spanish romances. Ticknor [4] calls the *Arcadia* a genuine pastoral romance, and its author " the true father of the modern prose pastoral." [5]

It was in imitation of the *Arcadia* that Montemayor wrote the *Diana*, the first Spanish pastoral romance.[6] That

---

[1] " Il vero maestre ed autore nel Sannazaro, colui al quale ci si diede, per sua salute, il suo dolcissimo padre, è Virgilio," p. lxxxi.

[2] *Ibid.*, p. ciii.

[3] *Ibid.*, p. cxi; and see p. cxii, where attention is called to the fact that Sannazaro was also indebted to other works of Boccaccio: the *Filocolo, Fiammetta, Ninfale fiesolano, Corbaccio* and the *Decamerone*.

[4] *History of Spanish Literature*, Boston, 1888, Vol. III, p. 93.

[5] For the great favor with which the *Arcadia* was received, various reasons have been assigned. Scherillo says: Se *l'Arcadia* fu accolta con tanto favore, ciò fu in gran parte perchè rappresentava la comune tendenza del tempo a quel sentimentalismo campestre, che pullula come per reazione nei periodi piu agitati delle armi: ed anche perchè richeggiava variamente le voci degli scrittori di quel mondo classico che tutti agognavano conoscere, in tanto fervore di rinascenza, come la più pura e più invidiata delle nostre glorie." l. c., p. ccxii.

[6] See Torraca, *Gl'Imitatori stranieri di Jacopo Sannazaro*, Roma, 1882, pp. 18, 19. A Spanish translation of the *Arcadia* appeared at Toledo in 1547, followed by a second, likewise at Toledo, in 1549.

the earlier and better Spanish romances followed their Italian models closely, is very clear; that their style, which is sometimes stilted and unnatural, is due to this close imitation, is, however open to question, though this reason has been assigned by a competent authority.[1]   For the Spanish

Nicolas Antonio mentions one at Toledo in 1554, and editions appeared in 1569, Madrid and Salamanca, Salamanca, 1578 and Madrid, 1620. As the *Diana* was certainly not begun until after 1554, Montemayor could have read the *Arcadia* in either one of the first three editions, though it cannot be doubted that he knew Italian. That, like all Spanish poets of his time, he read Petrarch, is certain, and Menéndez y Pelayo, (*Orígenes,* I. p. cdlxvii) observes that the *cancion;* " Aquella es la ribera, este el prado," (*Diana,* Bk. I.) is founded in part upon Petrarch's *Chiare, fresche e dolci acque.* It has been asserted by no less an authority than Dr. Carolina Michaëlis de Vasconcellos that the *Menina e Moça* of Bernardim Ribeiro, which first appeared in print at Ferrara in 1554, moved Montemayor to write his *Diana,* and this assertion is repeated by the distinguished scholar Sr. Menéndez y Pelayo, who says: " Que Montemayor conocía la obra de Bernaldim Ribeiro antes de emprender la suya es cosa que para mí no admite duda." (*Orígenes,* I, p. cdlxiv.)   And again: " La *Diana* en su fondo debe más al bucolismo galaico-portugués que á la *Arcadia*" (*Ibid.,* II, p. cxxxviii). Montemayor was the friend of Ribeiro and undoubtedly knew his *Saudades.* Braga' says: As relações pessoaes entre Bernardim Ribeiro e Jorge de Monte-Mór, que se descobrem pelas Eclogas d'aquelle bucolista, vem explicar-nos agora a influencia que a *Menina e Moça* exerceu na creação da *Diana.* Jorge de Monte Mór escreveu a historia dos seus amores infelizes em castelhano, e ainda que a sua obra seja uma das mais notaveis de litteratura hespanhola, pertenece-nos pela naturalidade do poeta e pela origem da sua imitação." (*Manual da Historia da Litteratura Portugueza,* p. 355; and see *Bernardim Ribeiro e os Bucolistas,* pp. 76 *et seq.*) That, on the other hand, Montemayor knew the *Arcadia* and was greatly influenced by it, must be equally clear to anyone asquainted with both works. See Torraca, *op. cit.,* p. 18. For an identification of the real personages hidden beneath the allegory of *Menina e Moça,* see Theophilo Braga, " Nueva Luz historica sobre Bernardim Ribeiro," in *Revista Crítica de Historia y Literatura Españolas,* Vol. I, p. 116 ff.

[1] See the Introduction to the Spanish Academy's edition of Valbuena's *Siglo de Oro,* Madrid, 1821.   Torraca also detects in the

pastoral romances, written originally for the amusement of courtiers, and artificial in their origin, remained so to a great extent in their general style and construction, and though such peculiar and distorted sentences not infrequently occur, in which the learned Spanish critic thinks he can detect the more free arrangement of word and phrase permitted by Italian syntax, yet such passages are easily outweighed by those in which the style is graceful and flowing. It must be admitted, however, that though some of the Spanish pastoral romances attained a very high degree of excellence, they are generally wanting in that idyllic simplicity and truth to nature which we find in the *Arcadia* of Sannazaro. They often indulge in the utmost extravagances and inconsistencies, introducing courtiers in the guise of shepherds, but whose refinements of speech at once betray them, so that, in many cases, the fact that the personages appear under the names of shepherds, is all that is left to indicate the pastoral character. This expedient of portraying living persons in a pastoral disguise, was not, however, an invention of the later writers, but had been used by Virgil in his Eclogues, in which the shepherds are often distinguished men of his time, while the poet himself often figures in them as an actor—a circumstance that has also been followed by most of the Spanish writers.[1] Moreover, many of the scenes and incidents described by the latter are such as never could be realized in nature, but are possible only in that imaginary Arcadia where the shepherds watched their "visionary flocks".

That the Spaniards were aware of the extravagances of

"prosa fiorita e cadenzata del Montemayor" the influence of the *Arcadia*.

[1] Also by English poets, among others by Spenser, in his *Colin Clout's come Home again*.

their romances and of their violence to the truth, there is abundant proof in their writings,[1] yet the device, for example, of introducing well-known poets or nobles as shepherds, doubtless added piquancy and color to the otherwise wearisome recitals of the *pastores,* especially in the eyes of those classes for whom they were chiefly written, and for whom it must have afforded no little amusement to discover —pictured beneath the thin veil of disguise, either their friends or themselves.

Of the popularity of this species of fiction among the upper classes,—for it was distinctly aristocratic in tone and not intended for the *profanum vulgus,*—there can be no doubt. It would also seem that the climate and the warm, impressionable nature of the people, were not unimportant factors in its success, since pastoral poetry never flourished to such an extent in northern countries, for lack of conditions congenial to its growth.

[1] See the *Galatea* of Cervantes, below.

THE " DIANA " OF MONTEMAYOR

The pastoral romance was introduced into Spain by
George de Montemayor, whose *Diana* was the first, and
still ranks as one of the best examples of this species of
prose fiction in the literature of Spain. Its success soon
brought forth a host of imitators,[1] for no book in Spain

[1] The *Diana* was imitated not only in Spain, but also in other countries. To discuss these imitations, however, is beyond the scope of
the present essay. It will suffice to mention two of the most famous:
the *Arcadia* of Sir Philip Sidney (1590) in England, and the *Astrée*
of Honoré d'Urfé (1610) in France. In both these romances all the
defects of the *Diana,* some of which will be noted further on (*cf.* p.
23), appear in an exaggerated degree; and however dull some of the
Spanish romances may be, they all possess, in comparison with the
ponderous *Arcadia* and the five thick tomes (1610-1627) of the *Astrée,*
at least the merit of brevity. I am aware that Menéndez y Pelayo
says: " Con poca razón cuentan algunos entre las imitaciones de la
Diana la *Arcadia* de Sir Felipe Sidney, que por su título recuerda á
Sannazaro y por su desarrollo es más bien un libro de caballerías
que una verdadera pastoral." *Orígenes de la Novela,* I, p. cdlxxvi.
I admit the truth of the latter part of this statement, nevertheless, the
influence of the *Diana* upon the *Arcadia* is unmistakable. Whatever
of Sidney's style may be due to Euphuism, which he condemns in
his *Apologie for Poetry,* it seems certain to me that it is not an imitation of Sannazaro, but often greatly resembles the peculiar diction
of Montemayor. Compare the opening passages of the *Diana* with
those of the *Arcadia,* " Ay memoria mia, enemiga de mi descanso! "
with " remembrance, restless remembrance," etc., or other passages
in the *Diana,* book i, with this, taken at random from the *Arcadia,*
book iii : " Then Musidorus, as contented as one who had been brought
from hell to heaven, with many vehement attestations to win trust
with her, and imprecations against himself in case of perjury, wished,
if ever his mind were so unhappy as to be surprised by any purpose
tending in the least degree to grieve her, that he might never live till
it took effect, but die e'er it were discovered." Prof. Fitzmaurice-
Kelly says that Montemayor's Felismena is the prototype of Sidney's

18

since the appearance of *Amadis of Gaul* ...d been received with the favor that was bestowed on the *Diana*.

Of its author, George of Montemayor, little is known: we neither know his name nor the date of his birth.[1] He was a Portuguese, born at Montemôr o Velho, a town on

Daïphantus. *The Relations between Spanish and English Literature,* Liverpool, 1910, p. 19. Sidney evidently read the *Diana* with pleasure and knew it well. He translated two lyrics from the first book: *Cabellos, quanta mudança:* "What changes here, O haire," and *De merced tan estremada:* "Oft this high grace with bliss conjoyn'd," and shows everywhere his intimate acquaintance with the Spanish pastoral. Speaking of Sidney's Arcadianism, the successor of Euphuism, Landmann says: "Sidney certainly avoided Euphuism, but he brought in another taste that led to the same exaggeration as North's translation [of Guevara] had led to in *Eupheus.* Sidney was the first to introduce into England the shepherd romance, with its flowery language and endless clauses, its tediousness and sentimentality, which characterize the shepherds of Sannazaro's *Arcadia,* from Montemayor's *Diana* to the *Astrée.* The Italian as well as the Spanish work shows an affected style of speech. Sidney was probably influenced by the diction of both, etc. *New Shakspere Society's Translations,* Series I, No. 9, p. 261. But the *Arcadia* is hardly a true pastoral romance; the action takes place in the highest classes of society, the chief figures being princes and princesses. Shepherds and shepherdesses play a very subordinate part, and while the influence of the *Diana* is of a general character, it is none the less clear to a careful reader. That Sidney's contemporaries had no doubt of the influence of the *Diana* upon the *Arcadia* is seen in the introductory letter to Sir Fulke Greville written by Thomas Wilson, the translator of the *Diana,* who says: Sr. Philipp Sidney did very much affect and imitate the excellent Author there of," i. e. of the *Diana.* On the relative influence of Spanish and Italian upon the English of Shakespeare's time, see Farinelli's review in *Revista Crítica de Historia y Literatura Españolas,* Vol. I, 1895, pp. 134 ff.

[1] See *Jorge de Montemayor, sein Leben und sein Schäferroman die " Siete Libros de la Diana,"* von Georg Schönherr, Halle, 1886, a very careful work to which I have several times referred. Every page of the introductory portion of Schönherr's work shows, moreover, his indebtedness to Mad. Carolina Michaëlis de Vasconcellos. To this friend, whose kindness is as unfailing as her learning, I also owe much in this chapter on Montemayor.

the right bank of the Mondego, about four leagues from Coimbra. It is probable that he was born between 1520 and 1524. For an account of his early years,—very vague it must be confessed,—we are indebted chiefly to his letter to Sâ de Miranda, a sort of autobiography, written in 1553, while Montemayor was temporarily residing at the Portuguese court.[1] In it he tells us that his youth was passed on the banks of the Mondego,[2] and that the education he acquired was very slight. We are told by his friend and continuator, Alonso Perez,[3] that he knew no Latin, at a time when that language was studied by all who made any claim to culture. But he had a good knowledge of the earlier as well as the contemporary Spanish, Portuguese, Catalan and Italian poetry, which was certainly not to the detriment of his Muse.

Montemayor's early years, he himself tells us, were devoted chiefly to music, though while still a youth he practiced the art of poetry. When quite young he left his

[1] " Carta de Jorge de Montemayor," in *Poesias de Francisco de Sâ de Miranda*, edited by Carolina Michaëlis de Vasconcellos. Halle, 1885, p. 665. See Appendix.

[2] By the waters of this historic stream Camões also passed his early years. See his one hundred and eleventh sonnet, beginning: " Doces e claras aguas do Mondego." Camões's birthplace is uncertain, but Storck inclines to Coimbra as his native city. " Luis Vaz'de Camoens Geburtsort ist mit völliger Sicherheit nicht festzustellen, aber doch mit grösster Wahrscheinlichkeit." *Luis'de Camoens Leben*, Paderborn, 1890, p. 102. The year of his birth was probably about 1525. *Ibid.*, p. 136.

[3] In the *Segunda Parte de la Diana*, in the address to the Reader, he alludes to Montemayor's lack of *letras Latinas*. But the statement of this pedant should not be taken literally. Montemayor certainly knew some Latin, as his *Cancionero* amply shows. It is quite certain, however, that he was never enrolled at any University. Lope de Vega praises Montemayor in his *Laurel de Apolo* (fol. 26, ed. of 1630). The verse: " si le ayudaran letras el ingenio," may be due to Perez.

native land " to make his own living, somehow or other "
(*por algun modo*), and turned his footsteps toward Spain.
As already observed, we do not know the family name
of Montemayor. It has been conjectured that he must have
been related in some way to the family of Payva y Pina [1]
However this may be, his parents must have been very
poor. His father seems to have been a silversmith (*platero*) and probably of jewish extraction. [2]

Further evidence of the humble condition of Montemayor's parents is furnished by a document discovered by
Sr. Sousa-Viterbo. It is a letter to the Queen of Portugal,
Da. Catharina, wife of D. João III., requesting her aid in

[1] In an elegy on the death of Montemayor by a contemporary, Marcos Dorantes, and which is found in many of the later editions of the
Diana, we read:

> "Los de Payua y de Pina y su nobleza
> demuestren quanto mas justo les fuera
> morir que no dar muestra de tristeza"
> P. 354, ed. of Lisbon, 1624.

This conjecture, as Schönherr remarks, is further confirmed by a
reference in the eighth stanza of Montemayor's poem *La Historia de
Alcida y Syluano* in which the poet figures under the name Syluano.
Here we read:

> "Baxo los altos pinos muy umbrosos
> con los de Pina siempre conuersaua,
> cuyo linaje y hechos generosos
> al son de su çampoña los cantaua.
> Y los de Payua alli por muy famosos
> sus virtudes heroycas celebraua," etc. P. 242.

[2] So, at least, we are to infer from some satirical verses by Juan
de Alcalá, a stocking maker (*calcetero*), of Seville, "muy gentil poeta,"
whose verses are printed by Menéndez y Pelayo (*Orígenes de la
Novela Española,* Vol. I, pp. cdlxviii and cdlvii). Mad. Carolina
Michaëlis de Vasconcellos writes me: " Vielleicht war sein Vater ein
vaternamens-loser illegitimer Sprösling jenes Hauses [i. e. Payva y
Pina], und die Mutter oder Grossmutter (?) eine spanische Sängerin
jüdischer Abkunft (?)." See also Gröber's *Grundriss,* II, 2 Abt., p.
304, note, and Schönherr, p. 16.

procuring an office from the King for the father of Monte-
mayor, whose name, however, is not given.[1]   This letter
Sr. Sousa-Viterbo correctly ascribes, not to the Infanta Da.
Maria, daughter of João III., who died in Valladolid on
July 12, 1545,[2] but to the King's daughter-in-law, the
Princess Da. Joanna.   It bears no date, but is endorsed
1557.

The first information we possess of Montemayor as an
author is in 1545, when he made his literary debut in Lisbon.[3]   Upon the death of the Infanta Da. Maria, which

---

[1] The letter is as follows: " Señora: Monte maior tiene ay a su
padre y desea mucho que el Rey my señor le haga merced de un oficio
que pide: suplico a V. al. sea servida de aiudalle con su alteza pera
que le haga la merced que oviere lugar que pera my sera muy grande
toda la que V. al. le hiziere en esto.   Nuestro señor guarde a V. al.
como yo deseo—besa las manos a V. al. = la princesa.   Sobrescripto:
Reyna my Señora.   *Archivo historico portuguez* (1903), p. 256.   Sousa-
Viterbo, an excellent scholar, blind in his later years, died on January 20, 1911.

[2] On this Infanta Da. Maria, who never wore the crown of Spain,
see an interesting article by A. Costa Lobo, in the *Archivo historico
portuguez*, Vol. I (1903), pp. 131, 177 ff.

[3] Carolina Michaëlis de Vasconcellos, Gröber's *Grundriss*, II, 2 Abt.,
p. 304, note.
According to Sousa-Viterbo, Montemayor came to Spain in the
retinue of the Infanta Doña Maria, daughter of D. João III, who
left Portugal on October 10, 1543, and shortly thereafter married in
Salamanca Prince Philip, son of Charles V, who afterward became
Philip II. of Spain.   In this he is in error, as Mad. Vasconcellos informs me, who says, " Ueberhaupt halte ich die Tochter Johann's III
nicht mehr, wie ich früher that, für eine der Beschützerinnen des
Dichters, wie aus nachfolgenden Notizen hervorgeht."   After allud-
ing to the departure of the Infanta Maria from Spain in 1543, Mad.
Vasconcellos says: " Wesentlich scheint mir dass *nirgends* ein Wort
darüber verlautet dass Montemayor zu ihrem Gefolge gehörte.   Nicht
einmal in dem ausführlichen portug. Reisebericht, wo jeder musik-
alischen Aufführung Erwähnung geschieht.   Ueberhaupt weiss die
Geschichte von keiner einzigen Musikkapelle die eine portug. Fürstin
aus der Heimat mitbekommen hätte: weder Beatrix von Savoyen
(1526), noch Da. Isabel zu Karl V (1526),—die Königlichst aus-

took place at Valladolid on July 2, 1545, he wrote the beautiful *coplas* glossing the *Recuerde el alma dormida* of Jorge Manrique,[1] as well as a mediocre sonnet that afterwards appeared in his *Cancionero*. At this time Montemayor was still in Portugal,—in Lisbon doubtless, without office or employment.

The earliest dated work of Montemayor is his *Exposicion moral*,[2] published at Alcalá in 1548, and dedicated to

gestatteten Töchter Emanuels—noch vorher die Kaiserin Leonore. In Spanien besass man (seit Ferdinand und Isabella) vorzügliche Kapellen. Philip, besonders, bedurfte sicherlich nicht der Sänger u. Instrumentisten seiner Braut. Und wenn auch einer oder der andre vereinzelte Musiker von hier nach Spanien ging (siehe *Romances Velhos*)—Beispiele sind eben Montemór u. Gregorio Silvestre—so Kamen ungleich mehr von Spanien hierher. Ganze Kapellen mit Catharine (1527)—u. D. Juana (1551). Die Princesa D. Maria nahm 1543 (so weit ich sehe) wie ihre Tanten Beatrix u. Isabel ungeheuer viel Gold und Silbergerät, Teppiche, u. Stoffe als Aussteuer mit,—aber keine *Musicos*. Zu ihrer Kapelle nur: 6 namenlose *moços* (für den Altar u. Mess dienst) : Sämmtliche bei S. V. und in den *Provas* aufgeführten Listen betreffen die Princesa de Portugal, D. Juana, wie der Vergleich lehrt."

[1] Garcia Perez, *Catálogo de los Autores portugueses que escribieron en Castellano,* Madrid, 1890, p. 393. Montemayor, *Cancionero,* ed. 1554, fol. 36v. Mad. Carolina Michaëlis de Vasconcellos says that the *pliego suelto* in the National Library at Lisbon, which contains the above *glosas,* is without date, but certainly belongs to the year 1545 or at latest to 1546. " Die gleichzeitigkeit ergiebt sich, mehr als aus Montemór's z. T. recht schönen lyrischen Strophen, aus dem zweiten angeschlossenen bänkelsänger-artigen Bericht von Gabriel de Saravia (Año de mil y quinientos quarenta y cinco corria en el mes de Julio era y en Valladolid la villa) und aus M's noch recht ungelenkem *Prolog*. an den *Regidor de Portugal,* D. João da Silva, und aus der Tatsache dass der Dichter, statt Selbständiges zu schaffen, sich mit einer Glosse begnügte, schliesse ich dass wir es mit einem *Erstlingswerk* zu thun haben. Dass M. damals noch in Lissabon weilte geht aus Str. 5 hervor, wo er *d'esta Lisboa* (*esta ciudad* in Str. 6) spricht; aus anderen Bemerkungen dass er der Abreise D. Maria's (1543) beigewohnt hatte."

[2] *Exposicion moral sobre el Psalmo Lxxxvi del real propheta Dauid,*

the Infanta Doña Maria, the author describing himself as
"singer in the chapel of the Infanta Da. Maria." This
princess, the eldest daughter of Charles V., the sister of
Philip and of Da. Juana, was twenty-six years old in 1548,
and on September 17th of the same year was married to
Maximilian II. of Austria at Valladolid. In 1551 the latter
became King of Bohemia, (whither Da. Maria then accompanied him), and Emperor in 1564. After his death, in
1564, Da. Maria returned to Spain, where she died in 1603.
It is this Princess Da. Maria whom Montemayor celebrates
in the "Canto de Orfeo" (*Diana,* Book IV) as the great
Queen of Bohemia and Austria-Hungary, and as "Luz de
España." [1]

After the departure of Da. Maria for Bohemia in 1551,
or perhaps shortly before that time, Montemayor found
another patron, and his chief one, in her sister, the Princess
Da. Juana of Castile, into whose service he then entered.
This is shown by a document published for the first time by
Sr. Sousa-Viterbo, in which D. João III. bestows upon
Montemayor "servant of the princess, my much beloved
daughter" a clerkship upon a vessel. [2] Sousa-Viterbo says

---

*dirigido a la muy alta y muy poderosa señora la infanta doña Maria
por George de monte mayor cantor de la capilla de su alteza.* Colophon: Esta presente obra fue vista y examinada por el muy reuerendo
y magnifico señor el vicario general en esta metropoli de Toledo y
con su licencia impressa en la universidad de Alcala por Joan de
Brocar: primero del mes de Março de MDXLVIII. 4°.

[1] See also Montemayor, *Cancionero,* ed. 1554, fol. 25.

[2] Eu el Rey faço saber a vos feytor e oficiaes das casas da Imdia
e Myna, que ey por bem e me praz de fazer merce a Jorge de Momte
Moor, criado da princesa mynha muito amada e prezada filha, da
escreuanynha de hũu dos nauios da carreira da Myna por hũa viagem
por ida e vinda e com ho ordenado cõtheudo no Regimento de pois de
cõpridas as prouisões que das taes escreuanynhas tiuer pasadas a outras
pesoas feytas amtes deste. Noteficoulo asy e mamdo que tamto que
pela dita maneira ao dito Jorge de Mõte mor couber ētrar na dita

that it is evident that the King here applies the word daughter to his daughter-in-law, the Princess Doña Juana. In the same Archives there is another document giving a list of the singers and musicians in the chapel of the Infanta Doña Juana, in which we find the names of Miguel Frances de Carenina, Alfonso de Renteria, Antonio de Vilhadiego, Jorge de Môtemor, and others, who are each to receive 40,000 maravedis yearly.[1] Montemayor's name appears in another list of the musicians in the chapel of Doña Juana, which is also published by Sousa-Viterbo.[2] Here, likewise, he received 40,000 maravedis annually. On December 5, 1552, the Princess Da. Juana married the crown prince of Portugal, D. João, son of João III. After her marriage she went to Portugal with her husband, Montemayor returning with her from Valladolid, and was

escreuanynha o metaes em pose dela e lhe deyxes ir seruir e aver o dito ordenado como dito he, e os proes e precalços que lhe dereytamente pertemcerem sem nyso lhe ser posto duvida nem ēbargo algũu, por que asy he mynha Merce, e ele jurara na chancelaria que bem e verdadeiramente a syrua. Antonio de Mello o fez em Almeirim a xiiij dias de março de jbclj. Amdre Soarez o fez escrepver. (Torre do Tombo, Chancellaria de D. João 3°. Doações, liv. 62, fl. 167). *Archivo Historico Portuguez* (1903), p. 256. " Hier belohnte man ihn (spät 1551) mit dem *Schreiberposten* (den er der Sitte entsprechend) für Geld an einen andern hätte abtreten können."—C. M. de Vasconcellos.

[1] Sousa-Viterbo, *ibid.*, p. 257. The papers are marked: " Papeles da Embaxada de Inglaterra e da jornada de Castella sobre a yda da Iffa. Donna Maria. Com outros varios todos do tempo do sr. Lco. Pirez de Tauora." Though the name here given is Da. Maria, Mad. Carolina Michaëlis de Vasconcellos says: " Es bedarf nur eines Vergleiches zwischen den Listen Sousa-Viterbo's und den *Trovas* (see below) um zu erkennen dass die Kapelle der Princesa Da. Juana gemeint ist."

[2] Rol dos creados e pessoas que agora tem a Senhora Princeza Donna Joanna filha do Emperador o qual rol mandou a El Rey Nosso Senhor Lourenço Pirez de Tavora, sendo Embaixador." *Archivo Historico Portuguez* (1903), p. 257.

apousentador in her household, receiving the same salary. The poet alludes to this service in his letter to Sâ de Miranda.[2]

The Prince D. João died on January 2, 1554, and on January 20 Da. Juana gave birth to a posthumous son, afterward the unfortunate King Sebastão. On May 16, she left Portugal, being called home by the Emperor to assume the regency during the absence of Philip in England (July 13, 1554, till September, 1555) and while he was in Flanders and France, whence he did not return till 1559. On this return journey of Da. Juana to Valladolid, Montemayor was in her retinue, as we have just seen. In the stanza of the *Canto de Orfeo* relating to the Princess Doña Juana, Montemayor refers to the death of her husband, "espejo y luz de Lusitanos." This part of the *Diana* could, therefore, not have been written before 1554. In the next stanza "la gran Doña Maria, de Portugal infanta soberana" was the daughter of Emanuel and his third wife Eleonore,[3] and the allusion to the death of the latter

---

[1] "Memoria das pessoas que veiram com a Princeza Da. Joanna.— Jorge de Montemayor, tem por meu apousentador outro tanto (scil. 30 milreis de ordenado) e maes lhe hão de dar dez mil reis para ajuda de custa por alvará meu aparte, que dando—lhe satisfaçam d'elles os não aja d'ahi em diante, e he todo o que ha de haver carenta mil reis." Antonio Caetano de Souza: *Provas da Historia Genealogica da Casa Real Portugueza,* Lisbon, 1744, p. 75, quoted by Schönherr, p. 22, n.

[2] See Appendix, ll. 43-48, of the fragment there printed: also the poem: *Al Principe de Portugal,* in his *Cancionero,* ed. 1554, fol. 15.

[3] D. Leonor was the third wife of D. Manoel and the sister of Charles V. and of Maria of Hungary. Speaking of the orphan children D. Maria and D. Catharina of the Infante D. Duarte (1515-1540), Mad. Carolina Michaëlis de Vasconcellos says: "Ouçamos o cysne de Montemór que as avistou no paço da Rainha, ao lado da Infanta [Maria], nos festas do Noivado de D. João e D. Juana (1552). Ao dar á luz a sua obra-prima, o romance pastoril de Diana, pendurou os retratos das duas meninas num d'esses Templos de Gloria em que era

n 1558, gives us another date before which the *Diana*
ould not have been written. It was to Prince D. João
nd to the Princess Da. Juana that Montemayor dedicated
his *Cancionero*, which first appeared at Antwerp in 1554; [1]
it is probable that he passed the latter part of 1553 or the
early months of 1554 in Antwerp, seeing his book through
the press.

Sometime between 1543 and 1552 Montemayor resided
at Seville, where he was on terms of intimacy with the poet
Gutierre de Cetina, as an exchange of sonnets between
them shows.[2]   Nicolas Antonio, followed by Sedano and
others, thinks that Montemayor accompanied Philip II. on
his visit to England and the Netherlands in 1554.[3]   Of
this there is no positive evidence, but there is *some,* and

---

praxe collocar celebridades coevas.   Primeiro a Infanta, no momento
em que a perda da mãe [i. e. Eleonore] a perturbou profundamente:

"Mirad, Ninfas, la gran doña Maria," etc.

In a note, the authoress adds: "A allusão á morte de D. Leonor
serve para determinarmos a data 1558 como termo *a quo* da conclusão
e publicacão da *Diana.*"   See the very interesting work: *A Infanta
D. Maria de Portugal* (1521-1577).   Porto, 1902.

[1] *Las Obras de George de Monte mayor, repartidas en dos Libros,
y dirigidas a los muy altos y muy poderosos señores don Juã y doña
Iuana, Principes de Portugal* [device].   *En Anuers. En casa de Iuan
Steelsio, Año de MDLIIII. Con priuilegio Imperial.*   Colophon: Fue
impresso en Anuers, en casa de Juan Lacio, 1554, sm. 12°, xii + 257 ff.
I possess the Salvá copy of this very rare work.

[2] "Soneto de Gutierre de Cetina, siendo enamorado en la Corte
para donde Montemayor se partia."   *Cancionero,* ed. 1554, fol. 35v.
"Responde Montemayor siendo enamorado en Seuilla, adonde Gutierre
de Cetina quedaua."   *Ibid.,* fol. 36.   Cetina addresses him as *Lusitano,*
a name Montemayor adopts in his poems.

[3] Philip II. set sail from Coruña on July 13, 1554, and arrived at
Southampton on the nineteenth or twentieth of the same month.   He
remained in England fourteen months, going thence to the Netherlands, and returned to Spain on August 2, 1559.   Watson, *History of
Philip II.,* Vol. I, p. 131.

slight as it is, it has not hitherto been mentioned, so far a
I know.   It is found in the reply of Montemayor to a lette
of his friend, Sr. Peña, in which the lines occur:

> "Andaua el pobre amor buscando abrigo,
>   jamas le hallo, *God helpe,* le dezian." [1]

I think it will be generally admitted that it is most unusual
to find a Spanish poet of this period quoting English, and
this, taken in connection with the well-known fact that
Philip was accompanied by some of the best singers and
musicians of Spain, renders it highly probable that Montemayor was in his retinue.[2]   Moreover, the above is not
found in the edition of 1554, which strengthens the probability.[3]

---

[1] *Cancionero del excelentissimo poeta George de Monte mayor: de
nueuo emendado, y corregido.   Dirigido al Illustrissimo Señor Gon-
çalo Fernandez de Cordoua, Duque de Sessa, y de Terra noua, Marques de Bitonto, Conde de Cabra: señor de la casa de Vaena.   En
Salamanca, En casa de Domingo de Portonrijs, impressor de la
Magestrad Real,* 1571.   This volume was kindly loaned to me by my
friend, Dr. Horace Howard Furness.   In the dedication, Montemayor
begs the Duke to receive the work "debaxo de su amparo, como el
autor dello ha estado siempre," etc.   This was the third Duke of Sessa,
in whom we find another patron of our poet.   The lines quoted above
are found on fol. 175 of this edition.   In the ed. of Alcalá, 1563, they
occur on fol. 165.

[2] Of the Spanish poets who accompanied Philip II., the name of
only one is known to me with certainty: "Juan Verzosa was in the
suite of Philip II, and composed, in celebration of the King's wedding
with Mary Tudor, the 'Epithalamie or nuptiall song' mentioned in
The Art of English Poesie, by George Puttenham.   This poem, however, was written in Latin (see Bartolomé José Gallardo, *Ensayo de
una biblioteca de libros raros y curiosos,* tomo iv, no. 4507).   Verzosa's name is given correctly by William Vaughan in *The Golden
Grove.*   Puttenham prints 'Vargas'."   Fitzmaurice-Kelly, *The Relations between Spanish and English Literature,* Liverpool University
Press, 1910, p. 13, note.

[3] The letter of Sr. Peña to which Montemayor's poem is an answer,

That Montemayor was living in the Netherlands in 1557-558 is shown by the dedication of his *Segundo Cancionero piritual*, published in Antwerp in 1558.[1] In the King's rivilege Montemayor is styled " servant of the most serene ?rincess of Portugal, his sister "; he was still, as we see,

s thus entitled: " Esta Carta embiaron a Montemayor en Flandes," which again agrees with the known facts. In this poem our poet men-:ions Petrarch, Bembo and Sannazaro, with whose writings he was :ertainly well acquainted. Indeed, in the *Cancionero* of 1554, fol. 37v, is found the following close imitation of a well known sonnet of Petrarch :

> " Dichoso a sido el año, el mes, y el dia,
> la hora, y el momento que en mirarte
> silencio puso amor en mi alegria."

From the evidence given above, it is possible that some of the *coplas* written by poets who accompanied Philip II to England, in 1555, may be by Montemayor. *Cf. Cancionero General*, II, p. 597:

No. 279. *Cancion*

Que no quiero amores
en Inglaterra,
pues otros mejores
tengo yo en mi tierra, etc.

No. 280. *Cancion*

¡ Ay Dios de mi tierra,
Saquéysme de aqui!
¡ Ay que Inglaterra
ya no es para mi, etc.

Evidence of the fact that our poet was in the service of Philip II, in 1554, is found in the " Soneto de Francisco de Soto, musico de Camara de su Magestad," in which he alludes to Montemayor as :

> " . . . . . muy excellente trobador
> Nombrase en cas del Rey Monte mayor."

This Francisco de Soto is mentioned in both the lists of " Cantores y musicos " given above, in which our poet figures.

[1] It is well known that in all subsequent editions to the first (1554), the *Obras* of Montemayor were divided in two parts; in the next edition (Antwerp, 1558) the first part is entitled: *Segundo Cancionero de George de Monte mayor* (Salvá, *Catálogo,* Vol. I, No. 296) ; the second part: *Segundo Cancionero Spiritual de Iorge de Monte Mayor dirigido Al muy magnifico Señor Ieronimo de Salamanca* [device]. *En Anvers, En casa de Iuan Latio. MDLVIII. Con Priuilegio.* 12°, 251 pp. This latter part Salvá, apparently, had never seen. It is carefully described by Prof. Vollmöller in *Romanische Forschungen,* IV, p. 333.

in the service of the Princess Juana. In the dedication
the poet states that " he has been labouring many day
upon this book and communicating with many theologians
as well in these states of Flanders as in Spain."

The assertion has often been repeated that Montemayor
like most of the great Spanish poets, was also a soldier, and
it is supported by two sonnets, the one entitled " Yendose
el autor a Flandes "[1] and the other " Partiendose para la
guerra ".[2] The latter alludes to the war with France, and
as Menéndez y Pelayo observes, the only war of Philip II.
with France in which the poet could have taken part was
that of 1555-1559, memorable for the victory of San
Quintin.[3] That Montemayor was living in Valencia while
he was writing his *Diana* is exceedingly likely; many of the
ladies whom he celebrates in the *Canto de Orfeo* were resi-
dents of that city.

Montemayor died in Piedmont (in Turin?) on February 26, 1561, killed, as it seems, in a duel in some love
affair. That his death was sudden and violent, is shown,—
in addition to the testimony of Padre Ponce, to be cited
presently,—by the Elegy of Dörantes:

> " With tearful voice, O muse of mine now sing
>   The dire misfortune and the sad event,
>   The sudden death, grievous and violent
> Of Lusitano, for whom sorrowing
>   All nature is in pitiful lament,
>   And to the world your meed of sorrow bring."

And again:

---

[1] *Cancionero,* ed. 1571, fol. 60.

[2] *Ibid.,* fol. 59v. Neither of these sonnets is found in the ed. of
1554.

[3] *Orígenes de la Novela,* Vol. I, p. cdl.

"Rigorous and inexorable fate
Cut with disdain the sweet thread of his life
With death untimely and incompassionate." [4]

[4] "Comiença musa mia dolorosa
el funesto sucesso y desuentura,
la muerta arrebatoda y presurosa
de nuestro Lusitano a quien natura
oy llora con muy tierno sentimiento,
y representa al mundo su tristura."

*   *   *   *   *
*   *   *   *   *

La inexorable Parca y rigurosa
cortó con gran desden su dulce hilo,
con inmatura muerte y lastimosa. . . .

Ed. 1624, pp. 353, 355.

Some interesting gossip concerning Montemayor is given in the dedication written by Lourenço Craesbeeck to the edition of the *Diana* which he printed at Lisbon in 1624. He tells us that it was Montemayor's intention to celebrate in verse the discovery of the East Indies, but that death prevented, or rather that Vasco de Gama desired that the greatest empire in the world should be reserved for the greatest poet, i. e. for Camões. He continues: "So great was the fame of Montemayor that there was not a house in which the *Diana* was not read, nor a street in which its verses were not sung, nor a conversation in which its style was not extolled; everybody, however great, desired a personal acquaintance with its author, who was invited to that splendid entertainment which the Duchess of Sessa gave in her garden to the principal ladies of the Court. Montemayor, entering with some servants of the Duke, in whose house he was then lodged, the Duchess introduced him to her guests, who inquired about the beauty of *Diana,* about the grievous action of the shepherd in marrying her, and about other things in his book, to which he replied with many gallantries, not a little proud of such good-fortune. The Marquise of Camarasa asked him: Sr. Montemayor, if you write such pleasing things about rustic shepherds, what would you do if you were asked to write about this garden, of these fountains and these Nymphs which you see here? To which Montemayor replied: All these things, my lady, are matter rather for wonderment than for the pen. And the Marquise of Guadalcassar, who was present at the entertainment, being asked what pleased her most, answered: the conversation of Montemayor. Likewise, Montemayor being one day in the monastery of the city of Leon, where he was convalescing

It is probable that Montemayor passed the last two or three years of his life at the Court, then at Valladolid. That his life here was irksome to him he tells us in a letter to his friend, D. Iorge de Meneses, in which, moreover, he paints a picture of his surroundings, which is far from flattering to the Court set:

> " Envy alone doth move me, this believe,
>   More than all other cause, *that* should I write,
>   Seeing that thou this Court now mayest leave." [1]

Again:

> " A sea of discord is this Court, which brings
>   Profit to no man, save by basest means:
>   Hatred and envy, lying, murmurings."

Everything that he sees about him is false,—a mere pretense, a make-believe; there is no room for honest endeavour; all that his youth looked forward to, turns out a hollow sham. He has experienced the disillusionment that comes with years, and he longs to be back once more in his native land, by the quiet waters of the Mondego of his youth. These longings he has here expressed with a simplicity and a charm that are indescribable, and which rank this poem among the very best that he has written. [2]

---

from an illness, he asked one of the fathers at Mass, to recite a gospel. To which he replied: I will say not one merely, but two, and reciting that of St. John, he continued—and now here is the other; that you are the most flowering wit of Spain."

[1] *Cancionero,* ed. 1571, fol. 74v. This *Epistola* is not in the edition of 1554.

> [2] " De la vida campestre ora tratemos,
>   en las riberas verdes nos metamos,
>   que todo lo demas olvidaremos.
>   Al campo de Mondego nos salgamos,
>   Al pie del alto fresno, sobre el rio
>   que los pastores tanto celebramos.

The *Diana* is the principal work of Montemayor and the
ꞁe by which he is best known. The year in which it ap-
ꞁeared is not certain, as the first edition printed at Valencia,
ꞁ undated. In all probability it issued from the press in
559.[1] In this year, as we are told by Fray Bartholomé

> Iamas te olvidaré, Mondego mio,
>   ni aun olvidarte yo sera en mi mano,
>   sino fuesse por muerte o desuario.
> En tu florido campo muy ufano,
>   tu dulce primauera quien la oluida,
>   sino quien a si proprio es inhumano?
> Aquella alta arboleda, aquella vida
>   que a su sombra el pastor cansado lleua,
>   y el aue oye cantar de amor herida.
> Aquel ver madurar la fruta nueua,
>   aquel ver como está granado el trigo,
>   y el labrador quel lino a empozar lleua." (fol. 76.)

[1] *Los siete Libros de la Diana de Iorge de Montemayor, dirigidos
al muy Illustre señor don Ioan Castella de Vilanoua, señor de las
baronias de Bicorb, y Quesa.* [Oval device: En una fe tostemps.]
Impresso en Valencia. 4°, iv + 112 ff. (Salvá, *Catálogo*, Vol. II, p.
167. It bears neither date nor printer's name, but Salvá says: "la im-
primió positivamente *Joan Mey*.") I have again (1910) examined
the copy in the Ticknor library, Boston, which bears the factitious
date 1542. I am now convinced that it was done with a pen. See the
note in the Ticknor Catalogue, p. 234, where the opinion is expressed
that "this date was foisted into the title-page when it was sold."
The next earliest dated edition known bears on the title-page: "Agora
nueuamente añadido de ciertas obras del mismo autor, y con diligencia
corregido. (At the end:) Fue impressa la presente obra en la muy
noble y leal ciudad de Caragoça, en casa de Pedro Bernuz. . . . Aca-
bose a veinte de Agosto, año 1560." Small 8°. It contains "*La Historia de Alcida y Sylvano,* compuesta por Iorge de Montemayor."
There is another, but undated edition, "In Milano por Andrea de
Ferrari, nel corso di porta Tosa," described by Menéndez y Pelayo,
Orígenes, Vol. I, p. cdlxii, which may belong to the same year.
Four editions appeared in 1561: Anvers, por Iuan Stelsio; Barcelona,
por Jayme Cortey; Cuenca, por Juan de Canova, and Valladolid, por
Francisco Fernandez de Cordoba. Of these I possess the Antwerp
edition; it does not contain the story of Abindarraez, which was first
added in that of Valladolid, 1561-62. A bibliography, containing all

Ponce,[1] that Montemayor was in Valladolid, then the Cou
of Spain " when everybody was reading the *Diana.*" Suc
popularity certainly implies a recent appearance of th
work.

Whether the lady whose praises Montemayor sings i
his *Cancionero* under the name of ' Marfida ' is identica
with the ' Diana ' of his pastoral romance, there is n
means of determining with certainty. I am inclined to be
lieve that she is not.[2] Lope de Vega tells us that " th
Diana of Montemayor was a lady of Valencia de Do1

editions as late as that of Lisbon, 1624 (which I also possess), wil
be found in Menéndez y Pelayo, *Orígenes,* Vol. I, p. cdlxiii; see alsc
Schönherr, pp. 80 ff. The only other important work of Montemayo1
(besides those previously mentioned), is his translation of the Catalan
poet Ausias March, which probably appeared at Valencia, before
1560. Salvá, *Catálogo,* Vol. I, p. 275. It is of this work that Lope
de Vega says: " Castissimos son aquellos versos que escriuió Ausias
March en lengua Lemosina, que tan mal y sin entenderlos Montemayor
traduxo." *Hermosura de Angelica,* Madrid, 1602, fol. 338v.

[1] *Primera parte de la Clara Diana a lo diuino, repartida en siete
libros. Compuesta por el muy Reverendo Padre fray Bartholome
Ponce. En Caragoça, Impressa por Lorenço de Robles. Año 1599.*
8°. There was an edition at Epila, 1580. Salvá, *Catálogo,* II, No.
1944. In the *prólogo* he says: " Being at the Court of Philip II, in
1559, I saw and read the *Diana* of Montemayor, which was at that
time in such favor as I had never seen any book in the vernacular.
Expressing a desire to know the author, I was introduced to him at
the house of a friend. Taking courage to tell him that he was wasting
time and talents in making rhymes and composing books of love,
Montemayor, with a hearty laugh, replied: Padre Ponce, let the friars
do penance for all; as for the *hijosdalgo,* arms and love are their profession. . . . May God have mercy on his soul, for I never saw him
again. A few months after this, I was told how a good friend of
his had killed him on account of jealousy, or some love-affair."

[2] Menéndez y Pelayo also leans to the belief that they were different
persons. *Orígenes,* Vol. I, p. cdli. Schönherr, *op. cit.,* is of the contrary opinion. I may add that the 1554 ed. of the *Cancionero* contains but two eclogues, while the later editions have four. In the
" Egloga tercera a la señora Doña Isabel osorio," the characters are

uan, near Leon, and its stream, the Ezla, and the lady will
e immortal through his pen." [1] This agrees not only with
he romance, but also with the story related by Faria i
Sousa,[2] according to which she is said to have been still
living in that town in 1602, when she was visited by Philip
he Third and Queen Margaret. She is described as even
hen bearing traces of her former beauty, though more than
sixty years old. This would fix her birth somewhere about
1540, and would, of course, effectually dispose of the belief
that an edition of the *Diana* existed as early as 1542, when
the heroine was only two years old.[3]

The story of the *Diana* is briefly given by the author in
his 'Argumento' as follows: "In the fields of the ancient
and celebrated city of Leon, by the banks of the river Ezla,
there lived a shepherdess named Diana, more beautiful than
any of her time. She loved and was loved in return by a
shepherd named Sireno, with a love chaste and pure. At
the same time she was loved by another shepherd, Silvano,
whom she, however, abhorred. It now happened that

Diana, Marfida, Danteo and Floriano. In the opening lines Diana
bewails the absence of Sireno: "Do estas, Sireno mio?" while Marfida is in love with Lusitano. Now, we know that Sireno is the poetical name assumed by Montemayor in the *Diana,* while the one he
adopts in his poems is Lusitano; so there is no inconsistency. As
the scene in this eclogue is also laid on the banks of "el claro rio
Mondego celebrado," (fol. 150v, ed. of 1571), it shows that Montemayor had already revolved the subject in his mind and that, very
probably, the *Diana* grew out of this eclogue.

[1] *La Dorotea,* Act II, Sc. II, fol. 52v, ed. of 1632.

[2] In his commentary on the *Lusiadas de Luis de Camões,* Madrid,
1639, Vol. II, col. 434, which is also related by Sepulveda, *Historia de
varios sucesos,* MS. Vol. II, Ch. XII. See *Bosquejo historico sobre
la Novela española,* by D. Eustaquio Fernandez de Navarrete, prefixed to Vol. 33 of the *Bib. de Aut. españoles* (p. xxvii, note).

[3] Since the first ed. of this book the whole matter has been reviewed by Fitzmaurice-Kelly, *Revue Hispanique,* II, p. 304, and see
also Menéndez y Pelayo, *Orígenes,* p. cdlix.

Sireno was obliged to leave the kingdom upon matter which admitted of no excuse. For a while Diana grieved on account of his absence, but as time changed, her heart changed also, and she was married to another shepherd named Delio. Sireno, returning after a year's absence, learns of her marriage, "and here begins the first book, and in the remaining ones you shall find various histories of things that have really happened, although disguised beneath a pastoral style."

It will be seen from this Argument that the *Diana* had its origin in an actual event in the life of its author, or so, at least, he leads us to infer, and that, perhaps, his principal object in writing it was to find expression for the sorrow and despair of a great disappointment, and thus obtain that relief and consolation which imparting our ills to others often gives.

"A raconter ses maux souvent on les soulage."[1]

It should be observed here, however, that it has been seriously doubted whether Montemayor is the protagonist of the *Diana,* and whether the love he relates has any basis in fact.[2]

---

[1] Or, in the words of Montemayor in an "Epistola" prefixed to the *Diana:* "Curar piensa sus males con dezillos."

[2] Menéndez y Pelayo, *Orígenes,* Vol. I, p. cdxlv. That, in the early years of the seventeenth century, the story of the *Diana* was generally believed to be founded upon an actual fact in Montemayor's life, can hardly be doubted. Upon this point the testimony of Lope de Vega, given above (p. 35) is clear. Lope's memory (he was born in the year following Montemayor's death) certainly reached back to a time when everything concerning our poet was vivid in the minds of educated men; indeed, Lope may have had his information from one who had personally known Montemayor. His own pastoral romance, the *Arcadia,* was begun about 1592, and we may well believe that his interest in the subject and in its celebrated exemplar, had long antedated this period. Craesbeeck, the Portuguese printer, tells

The form and construction of the *Diana* may have been matters of subordinate import to Montemayor, but a work is to be judged as it stands, and it must be admitted that the *Diana* is not without serious defects: many of its incidents are loosely interwoven; there is a lack of cohesion; the narrative is sometimes involved and is often interrupted by long digressions, so that the thread of the main story is lost and the interest flags. This want of logical development,—the failure to properly subordinate the various incidents of the story and thus hold the attention of the reader, is a fault conspicuous not only in the *Diana,* but in all Spanish romances of its class. Many of the incidents in the *Diana* are quite improbable, and its beauty is often marred by an excessive sentimentality, at times bordering on the ridiculous.[1] A few excerpts will illustrate this

us (see above, p. 31) that Montemayor had been ill for some time in the city of Leon, the scene of the *Diana*. It is fair to presume that this was a well-known tradition at the time, 1624. As to the story related by Faria y Sousa in 1639, we must admit that we should be on surer ground had it been vouched for by some more reliable chronicler. Faria says that the lady celebrated as Diana was named Ana, and that she was one of the wealthiest persons in Valencia de Don Juan. Mad. de Vasconcellos thinks that the name *Marfida,* under which Montemayor had celebrated his lady in his early poems, is an anagram of Margarida, but the name Marfida or Marfisa is found in Boiardo and Ariosto, and in the *Espejo de Caballerias,* which appeared at Seville in 1533, and occurs frequently both at this time and later. It is, probably, of no significance in the present inquiry. But as already stated above, the germ of the *Diana* is present in the third Eclogue of Montemayor, though I am inclined to think that Diana and Marfida are different persons.

[1] In this respect, however, the *Diana* was surpassed by some of the works that followed it. Sidney's *Arcadia* shows some remarkable passages: "The sun drew clouds up to hide his face from so pitiful a sight, and the very stone wall did yield drops of sweat for agony of such a mischief: each senseless thing had sense of pity; only they that had sense were senseless." (Book III, p. 537. ed. of 1743.)

A shepherd in despair exclaims: "O thrice happy I, if I had per-

" Venia pues el triste Sireno, los ojos hechos fuentes, e
rostro mudado y el coraçon tan hecho á desuenturas, que
si la fortuna le quisiera dar algun contento, fuera meneste:
buscar otro coraçon nueuo para recibille."   (Book I.)

ished whilst I was altogether unhappy; then, when a dejected shep
herd offensive to the perfection of the world, I could hardly, being
oppressed by contempt, make myself worthy to be disdained, disdair
to be despised, despised being a degree of grace. O would to God
that I had died obscurely, whilst my life might still have lived famous
with others and my death have died with myself." (Bk. III, p. 598.)
Another shepherd complains: " O my dun-cow, I did think some evil
was towards me ever since the last day thou didst run away from me,
and held up thy tail so pitifully: did I not see an eagle kill a cuckoo,
which was a plain foretoken unto me, Pamela should be my destruction? O wife Miso, if I durst say it to thy face, why didst thou
suspect thy husband, that loveth a piece of cheese better than a
woman," etc. (Bk. IV, p. 731.) Or such verses as these, which can
add nothing to Sidney's reputation:

> As I my little flock on Ister bank
> (A little flock; but well my pipe they couth)
> Did piping lead, the sun already sank
> Beyond our world, and e'er I got my booth,
> Each thing with mantle black the night doth scoth;
> Saving the glow-worm which would courteous be
> Of that small light oft watching shepherds see.
>
> The welkin had full niggardly enclosed
> In coffer of dim clouds his silver groats,
> Ycleped stars; each thing to rest disposed,
> The caves were full, the mountains void of goats:
> The birds' eyes clos'd; closed their chirping notes.
> As for the nightingale, wood-musick's king:
> It *August* was, he deign'd not then to sing.   (Page 711.)

I have not read Sidney's *Arcadia* for many years, and no longer
have a stomach for such pastime. So I must confess that I am one
of those " degenerate readers of our day " to whom " the Arcadia
seems almost as tedious as Hazlitt thought it." (Fitzmaurice-Kelly,
The Relation between Spanish and English Literature, Liverpool, 1910,
p. 19.)

Love drives poor Silvano out of his senses:

" Pues como este pastor (Silvano) fuesse tan mal tra-
ado de amor, y tan desfauorecido de Diana, mil vezes la
asion le hazia salir de seso, de manera que hoy daua en
lezir mal de amor, mañana en alaballe: un dia en estar
edo, y otro en estar mas triste que todos los tristes," etc.
(Book II, fol. 45, ed. 1561.) Belisa is determined to be
wretched; she says: " Muy gran consuelo seria para tan
desconsolado coraçon como este mio, estar segura de que
nadie con palabras ni con obras pretendiesse darmele, porque la gran razon, o hermosas Nimphas, que tengo de biuir
tan enbuelta en tristezas como biuo, ha puesto enemistad
entre mi y el consuelo de mi mal; de manera que si pensasse
en algun tiempo tenelle, yo misma me daria la muerte."
(Fol. 96.)

Their tears augment the streams and cause the grass to
grow:

" Mas que ventura ha guiado tan hermosa compañia, a
do jamas se vio cosa que diesse contento? Quien pensays
que haze crescer la verde yerua desta ysla, y acrescentar
las aguas que le cercan, sino mis lagrimas? Quien pensays
que menea los arboles deste hermoso valle, sino la boz de
mis sospiros tristes, que inflamando el ayre, hazen aquello
que el por si no haria? Porque pensays que cantan los
dulces paxaros por entre las matas, quando el dorado Phebo
esta en toda su fuerça, sino para ayudar a llorar mis desuenturas? A que pensays que las temerosas fieras salen al
verde prado, sino a oyr mis continuas quexas?" (Fol. 97.)

The shepherds are so overcome by this recital that they
all weep: " Con tantas lagrymas dezia esto la hermosa pastora, que no hauia ninguno de los que alli estauan, que las
suyas detener pudiesse."

As the contents of Montemayor's romance have been

set forth by several writers,[1] a brief analysis will be sufficient here.

The ' forgotten ' Syreno, coming from the mountain districts of Leon, arrives at the delightful meadows watered by the Ezla, and muses upon " the happy time when, in these fields and by these lovely banks, he tended his flocks." Here he passed his days oblivious of the outer world till " cruel Amor " made him his slave. " Reclining at the foot of a beech tree, his eyes followed the beautiful banks until they rested upon the spot where first he had seen the beautiful, graceful and chaste Diana, in whom nature had united every perfection." " What his heart then felt, let him imagine who ever found himself amid sad memories." He thinks of the time when Diana swore eternal fidelity to him " with tears gushing from her lovely eyes like oriental pearls, as witnesses of what she felt within her heart, bidding him believe what she had told him so many times." He now draws forth from his breast a paper containing some threads of green silk and some locks of hair, " and such locks! and placing them upon the green grass, with many tears, he takes up his lute, not as joyfully as in the days when he was favored by Diana," and sings as follows:

> Cabellos quanta mudança
> he visto despues que os vi,
> y quan mal paresce ay
> essa color desperança.
> Bien pensaua yo, cabellos,
> (aunque con algun temor)
> que no fuera otro pastor
> digno de verse cabe ellos.
> Ay cabellos, quantos dias
> la mi Diana miraua,
> si os traya, o si os dexaua,
> y otras cien mil njñerias.

[1] See Dunlop's *History of Fiction;* Schönherr, already quoted, and Kressner, *Zur Geschichte der pastoral Dichtung,* in Herrig's *Archiv,* Vol. LXVI (p. 309).

Y quantas vezes llorando
(ay lagrimas engañosas)
pedia celos, de cosas
de que yo estaua burlando.

Los ojos que me matauan,
dezi, dorados cabellos,
que culpa tuue en creellos,
pues ellos me assegurauan?
No vistes vos que algun dia
mil lagrimas derramaua,
hasta que yo le juraua,
que sus palabras creya?

Quien vio tanta hermosura
en tan mudable subiecto?
y en amador tan perfecto,
quien vio tanta desuentura?
O cabellos, no os correys,
por venir de a do venistes,
viendome como me vistes,
en verme como me veys?

Sobre el arena sentada
de aquel rio, la vi yo,
do con el dedo escriuio:
antes muerta, que mudada.
Mira el amor lo que ordena,
que os viene a hazer creer
cosas dichas por muger,
y escritas en el arena. (Fol. 4.)

Replacing the " golden locks," he finds in his shepherd's scrip a letter, formerly written to him by Diana, which he reads, and " deeply sighing," says: " How could forgetfulness ever enter a breast whence such words have issued?" Sireno now observes another shepherd approaching, to whom he exclaims: " Alas! unhappy shepherd, though not so unhappy as I." It is the *desamado* Silvano, once the rival of Sireno, but who became his friend on learning that Diana returned the latter's love. Silvano takes up his pipe, and " sings with great sadness ":

Amador soy, mas nunca fuy amado:
quise bien y querre, no soy querido;
fatigas passo, y nunca las he dado;
sospiros di, mas nunca fuy oydo;
quexarme quise, y no fuy escuchado;
huyr quise de Amor, quedé corrido,
de solo oluido no podré quexarme,
porque aun no se acordaron d'oluidarme.

Yo hago a qualquier mal solo un semblante,
jamas estuue hoy triste, ayer contento;
no miro atras, ni temo yr adelante,
un rostra hago al mal, o al bien que siento;
tan fuera voy de mi como el dançante,
que haze a qualquier son un mouimiento,
y assi me gritan todos como a loco,
pero segun estoy, aun esto es poco.

La noche a un amador le es enojosa,
quando del dia atiende bien alguno,
y el otro de la noche espera cosa
qu'el dia le haze largo e importuno;
con lo que un hombre cansa, otro reposa,
tras su desseo camina cada uno,
mas yo siempre llorando el dia espero,
y en viendo el dia por la noche muero.

Quexarme yo de Amor es escusado,
pinta en el agua, o da bozes al viento,
busca remedio en quien jamas le ha dado,
que al fin venga a dexalle sin descuento;
llegaos a el a ser aconsejado,
diráos un disparate, y otros ciento;
pues quien es este Amor? Es una sciencia
que no la alcança estudio, ni esperiencia.

Amaua mi señora al su Sireno,
dexaua a mi, quiça que lo acertaua;
yo triste a mi pesar tenia por bueno
lo que en la vida y alma me tocaua.
A estar mi cielo algun dia sereno,
quexara yo de amor si le añublaua,
mas ningun bien diré que me ha quitado;
ved, como quitará lo que no ha dado?

No es cosa Amor, que aquel que no lo tiene
hallará feria a do pueda comprallo,
ni cosa que en llamandola se viene,
ni que le hallareys yendo a buscallo;
que si de vos no nasce, no conuiene
pensar que ha de nascer de procurallo,
y pues que jamas puede amor forçarse,
no tiene el desamado que quexarse.   (Fol. 6.)

Perceiving Sireno by the fountain, he draws near, and " they embrace each other with many tears." The two " unloved " lovers console one another. Silvano now relates how Diana at first pined during Sireno's absence,— how he had once observed her lying upon the ground weeping; how Diana then drew forth a small pipe, " and played so sweetly that the valley, the mountain, the river and the enamoured birds,—even the wild beasts of the dense wood were charmed." Afterwards, with tearful eyes, gazing into the clear fountain, she sang:

" Ojos, que ya no veys quien os miraua
   (quando erades espejo en que se via)
   que cosa podreys ver que os dé contento? "   (Fol. 12.)

Silvano, continuing, relates how, on approaching, he was invited by Diana to sit beside her. How he began to tell Diana of his love for her, whereupon she promptly interrupted him, saying: " If your tongue again dares to speak of your own affairs, and fails to speak to me of my Sireno, I shall leave you to enjoy this clear spring at your pleasure." On hearing this Sireno sighs and asks whether Diana is happy since her marriage with Delio, to which Silvano replies: " They tell me that she is not happy, for though Delio, her husband, is rich in the gifts of fortune, he is poor in the gifts of nature," etc., " for Delio cannot play, sing and wrestle, nor dance with the *mozas* on Sunday."

A sad shepherdess now draws near; it is Selvagia, the

friend of Diana, who, addressing the shepherds, says: "What are ye doing here, O unloved shepherds, in this green and delightful meadow?" A discussion follows upon the fickleness of woman, after which Selvagia relates how she was deceived by the false Alanio, and of the complications which arose in the love of a number of shepherds and shepherdesses; each is in love with some one who loves somebody else (*cada uno perdido por quien no le queria*). "It was the strangest thing in the world to hear how Alanio, sighing, would say: "Alas, Ismenia! how Ismenia said: Alas, Montano! and how Montano said: Alas, Selvagia! and how Selvagia said: Alas, my Alanio!" The latter, we are told, lost no time in punishing Ismenia, for, fixing his eyes upon Selvagia, he sang this *antiguo cantar:*

> "Amor loco, ay amor loco,
>   yo por vos, y vos por otro," etc.

The result of all this sighing is that Montano marries Ismenia. Having finished her story, "Selvagia began to shed copious tears, and the shepherds aided her therein, for it was an occupation in which they had great experience."

The second book opens with a long complaint of Selvagia's, after which she sings some *sestinas*. Silvano now appears, singing some *octavas* to the music of a lute; both sit down beneath the shade of a dense myrtle, and with many sighs and a fair amount of tears, they relate to each other their imaginary woes. To Silvano's query "perhaps thou knowest some remedy for our ills?" Selvagia answers: "I do know one, shepherd; it is to cease loving." The "forgotten" Sireno is now heard singing a sonnet, and scarcely had they greeted the new-comer and proceeded together to "the fountain of the Alders," when they heard several voices singing. Advancing cautiously, they perceive three nymphs, Dorida, Cynthia and Polydora. Dorida now sings of the love of Diana and Sireno, much to the astonishment of Sireno, who is concealed behind the trees. The whole story is sung in a long *cancion,* of which one of the strophes is as follows:

Diana speaks: Toma, pastor, un cordon
que hize de mis cabellos,
porque se te acuerde en vellos
que tomaste posesion
de mi coraçon y dellos.
Y este anillo as de lleuar
do estan dos manos asidas,
que aunque se acaben las vidas,
no se pueden apartar
dos almos que estan unidas.

Sireno gives to Diana his shepherd's crook and his lute, "to which he has sung to her a thousand *canciones,* recounting her perfections."

Thus: Ambos a dos se abraçaron,
y esta fue la vez primera,
y pienso fue la postrera,
por que los tiempos mudaron
el amor de otra manera.
Y aunque a Diana le dió
pena rabiosa y mortal
la ausencia de su zagal,
en ella misma halló
el remedio de su mal.   (Fol. 59v.)

Scarcely had Dorida finished her song, when three wild men, "very tall and ugly," rush out of the wood, seize the nymphs and bind their hands. Now the shepherds spring from their ambush and attack the giants with slings. The shepherds were getting the worst of the contest, when suddenly, out of the thick grove there appeared a maiden of wonderful beauty, who immediately sends an arrow through the heart of one of the giants, and finally slays them all. The nymphs turn out to be priestesses of Diana, and the rescuing maiden, whose name is Felismena, now relates her story. After a brief account of her early years, she informs us how, at the age of seventeen she was beloved by Don Felix, whose love, at first, she did not return. Don Felix sends a letter by Rosina, the maid of Felismena, which letter the latter rejects, saying: " If I did not observe who I am and what might be said, I should mark your face—which shows little modesty—so that it were easily known among all others. But since this is the first time, let what is done suffice, but beware the second time." " It seems to me," continued Felismena, " that I can still see that traitorous Rosina, who, with a friendly countenance, knew how to be silent, dissimulating her true feelings at my angry outburst, and with a feigned smile saying to me: I gave this letter to your grace so that we might both laugh over it, but not that you should get angry on account of it." Presently, however, a desire arose in Felismena to read the letter, though modesty forbade her ask her maid for it after what had occurred between them. And so the day passed till night, mid various thoughts. " And when Rosina," Felismena continues, " entered to disrobe me, at the time when I was wont to retire, heaven knows whether I wished that she should again importune me to receive the letter, but I did not wish to speak of it, and in order to see whether opening the way would be of any advantage, I said: And so, Rosina, Señor Don Felix was so bold as to write to me? To which she answered dryly: ' My lady, these are things that love brings with it; I beg you to forgive me, for if I had thought that it would anger you, I would rather have torn out my eyes.' That night was the longest that Felismena had ever passed."

" Day having come, and later than I had wished it, the prudent Rosina again entered to dress me, and deftly let

the letter fall upon the floor, and as I saw it, I said: what
is that that just fell? Show it to me. It is nothing, my
lady, said she. Show it to me, and do not make me angry,
or tell me what it is. Why, my lady, do you wish to see it?
It is the letter of yesterday. That is surely not so, said I;
show it to me; I will see whether you told the truth.
Scarcely had I spoken. when she placed it in my hand, and
I, though knowing it very well, said, truly it is not the same
and you must be in love with some one. I wish to read it,
and see what he writes to you."

The reading of this letter aroused the love in the bosom
of Felismena, who, " taking pen and ink," sent a letter to
Don Felix in reply. And so the lovers were happy for
some time, till it came to the knowledge of the father of
Felix, who sent him to the court of the great princess Au-
gusta Cæsarina, to gain some knowledge and experience
of the world.

Felismena, however, could not bear the separation, but
determined to do " what never woman thought of—to
dress in male attire, visit the court, and see him in whose
sight rested all my hope."

After a journey of twenty days she arrives at the court,
and on the very first night she had the opportunity of convincing herself of the unfaithfulness of her lover, for she
hears Don Felix singing a serenade to his mistress Celia.
Felismena now enters the service of Don Felix as a page,
under the name of Valerio, and soon gains the confidence
of his master to such a degree that the latter makes Valerio
his confidant, telling him of his love for Celia and reading
the contents of Celia's letters to him.

Celia having learned, meanwhile, that she was not the
first love of Don Felix, but that the latter had declared his
love to a lady of his native city, and had afterwards de-
serted her, refused to accept his attentions any longer, and

sent him the above-mentioned letters. Don Felix now sends a letter to Celia by his page Valerio, the result of which is that Celia falls deeply in love with the latter. The peculiar dilemma in which Valerio found himself (or herself), was suddenly resolved by the death of Celia, who, finding her love for Valerio unrequited, fell in a swoon, from which she never awoke. At this news Don Felix disappeared. Two years had elapsed since then, and during all this time Felismena has been in search of the faithless Don Felix. (End of Book ii.)

At the conclusion of Felismena's story all proceed to the temple of Diana, to find some solace for their sufferings. They had not journeyed long, when they came to a beautiful lake, in the midst of which was a small island upon which they saw a hut and a flock of sheep. Passing over the water "upon stones placed in a row," Polydoro enters the hut and finds a shepherdess sleeping therein, "whose beauty causes no less astonishment that if Diana herself had appeared before their eyes." "In the carelessness of sleep her foot, white and bare, protruded from her frock, but not so far that to the eyes of those who were looking on, it might seem *deshonesto*." "And from the many tears that, even while sleeping, rolled down her lovely cheeks," it seemed that sleep was no bar to her sad thoughts. The beautiful shepherdess is Belisa, who presently relates how an old shepherd named Arsenio, whose wife had died, fell in love with her. Arsenio, however, had a son Arsileo who, in addition to being handsomer than Arsenio, had the advantage of being somewhat younger. Arsileo is also a poet and writes the verses which his father, Arsenio, sends to Belisa. On discovering this, Belisa falls desperately in love with Arsileo, as a consequence of which Arsileo, while visiting Belisa one night, is unwittingly shot by his father, who, when he discovers his deed, kills himself. Since then Belisa wanders about only wishing for death. All the shepherds shed copious tears on hearing this tale, and invite Belisa to accompany them to Diana's temple. (End of Book iii.)

All finally arrive at a magnificent palace, where they are graciously received by the wise Felicia, who bids them have no fear of the ills that pursue them, as she has a remedy for them. Over the doorway of the palace, which is built of jasper, silver, and various marbles, are two nymphs bearing tablets of copper on which is the following inscription in letters of gold:

Quien entra mire bien como ha biuido,[1] etc.

Here they find an immense statue of Mars, and here are represented Hannibal, Scipio, Camillus, Horace, Varro, Cæsar, Pompey, Alexander the Great, the Cid, Fernan Gonçalez, Bernardo del Carpio and the Great Captain (Gonçalvo de Cordoba), etc. They enter a magnificent hall adorned with ivory and alabaster, and here, by a spring of pure silver, sits Orpheus, who touches his harp at the approach of the group and sings a song (*Canto de Orpheo*) in praise of famous Spanish women. Proceeding further they come to a spacious lawn, where they sit down, and having dined sumptuously, Felismena relates the story of Abindarraez. As already observed, this story was added to the *Diana* after the death of Montemayor. (End of Book iv.)

Felicia now proceeds to cure the lovers of their ills. She appears with two goblets of fine crystal, one of which she hands to Sireno and the other to Selvagia and the unloved Silvano, saying: "take this goblet, in which you will find the best remedy for all your past misfortunes." All three, on drinking, immediately fall asleep. When Felicia thinks

[1] *Cf.* below, p. 65.

the magic potion has had its due effect, she touches Sireno's head with a book, whereupon he awakes and is entirely cured of his love for Diana. So Silvano, on awakening, forgets entirely his former love for Diana, but becomes enamoured of Selvagia, who, in turn, forgetting Alanio, falls in love with Silvano. These three then return to their flocks, and now, for the first time we meet with Diana. The voice of a shepherdess is heard singing, and is recognized by Silvano. She sits by the fountain and sings:

> "Quando yo triste nasci,
> luego nasci desdichada;
> luego los hados mostraron
> mi suerte desuenturada," [1] etc.

But Sireno remains unmoved by her song, and they proceed on their way. Felismena now leaves the company, going homeward, and on her way sees a shepherd's hut, which she enters and finds therein Arsileo, the lover of Belisa, who had not been slain by the arrow of his father, as Belisa had supposed, but Alfeo, a great sorcerer and the rejected suitor of Belisa, had conjured up two spirits to represent Arsenio and Arsileo, and the whole scene in which Arsenio shoots his son,—merely out of revenge against Belisa. (End of Book v.)

Though quite freed of his love for Diana, yet, once, on coming to the spring of the Alders, Sireno thinks of the happy past and feels lonely, because at all times " the memory of a happy state causes a feeling of solitude in him who has lost it." [2] Then he sees the flocks of Diana

---

[1] Menéndez Pelayo (*Orígines de la Novela*, I, p. cdlxiv), says that this song was inspired by Bernardim Ribeiro's *romance* beginning " Pensando-vos estou filha," in his *Menina e Moça*, Lisbon, 1852, p. 91. See *Orígenes*, p. cdxli.

[2] " Y passando por la memoria los amores de Diana, no dexaua de causalle soledad el tiẽpo que la hauia querido. No porque entonces le

and her dogs, who fall down at his feet and show their delight at seeing him, " and if the power of the water which the sage Felicia had given him had not made him forget his love, perhaps nothing in the world could have prevented him from returning to her."

He now takes up his lute and sings:

> Passados contentamientos
> qué quereys?
> dexadme, no me canseys.
>
> Memoria, quereys oirme?
> Los dias, las noches buenas,
> paguélos con las setenas,
> no teneys mas que pedirme;
> todo se acabó en partirme
> como veys,
> dexadme, no me canseys.
>
> Campo verde, valle umbroso
> donde algun tiempo gozé,
> ved lo que despues passé,
> y dexadme en mi reposo;
> si estoy con razon medroso,
> ya lo veys,
> dexadme, no me canseys.
>
> Vi mudado un coraçon,
> cansado de assegurarme,
> fue forçado aprouecharme
> del tiempo, y de la occasion;
> memoria do no hay passion
> qué quereys?
> dexadme, no me canseys.
>
> Corderos, y ouejas mias,
> pues algun tiempo lo fuistes,
> las horas ledas, o tristes
> passaronse con los dias;
> no hagays las alegrias
> que soleys,
> pues ya no m'engañareys.

diesse pena su amor, mas porque en todo tiempo la memoria de un buen estado causa soledad al que le ha perdido." (Fol. 180.) Here " soledad " is evidently used in the sense of the Portuguese " saudade."

> Si venis por me turbar,
> no hay passion, ni haura turbarme;
> si venis por consolarme,
> ya no hay mal que consolar;
> si venis por me matar
> bien podeys,
> matadme y acabareys.[1]

Diana now appears, but Sireno is unmoved by her prayers; in tears she declares that the will of her father and her childish obedience had brought her to the hated union with Delio: but Sireno rejoices that he has been freed of his love, and with Silvano sings a song, laughing at their former folly, when both were suitors of Diana. At the conclusion of the song Diana was shedding copious tears, " and with a sigh, in company with which her soul seemed to have gone forth," she arose, and braiding her golden hair, disappeared in the valley. (End of Book vi.)

Felismena, on her journey, arrives at a beautiful city by a majestic river. It recalls to her mind the great city of Soldina, " her birthplace, from which Don Felix had caused her exile ". From the language of two shepherdesses, Armia and Duarda, whom she meets, she learns that she is in

---

[1] I append Bartholomew Yonge's translation of the first stanza:

> Passed contents
> O what mean ye?
> Forsake me now, and doe not wearie me.

> Wilt thou heare me, O memorie?
> My pleasant daies, and nights againe,
> I have appaid with sevenfold paine:
> Thou hast no more to aske me why,
> For when I went, they all did die,
> As thou dost see,
> O leave me then, and doe not wearie me.

Another gloss upon the first three verses was written by Vincente Espinel, *Diversas Rimas*, Madrid, 1591, fol. 128, and now printed in Böhl v. Faber, *Floresta*, I, p. 282.

Portugal, and that the city before her is Coimbra, " one of the most famous cities in all Europe ", and that it " is bathed by the crystalline waters of the Mondego ". And the castle before them is called in the Portuguese tongue ' Monte-Mor o Velho,[1] where force of genius, valor and courage have remained as trophies of the deeds which its inhabitants performed in the past,[2] and whose ladies and gentlemen are adorned with all virtues." While Felismena partakes of the repast offered by the shepherdesses, the voice of Danteo is heard singing:

> Sospiros, minha lembrança [3]
> não quer, porque vos não vades,
> que o mal que fazem saudades
> se cure com esperança.
>
> A esperança não me val
> pola causa em que se tem,
> nem promete tanto bem
> quanto a saudade faz mal:
> mais amor, desconfiança,
> me derão tal calidade,
> que nem me mata saudade,
> nem me dá vida esperança.
>
> Errarãose se queixarem
> os olhos com que eu olhei,
> porque não me queixarei
> em quanto os seus me lembrarem;
> nem poderá hauer mudança
> jámays em minha vontade,
> ora me mate saudade,
> ora me deixe esperança.

[1] The birth-place of Montemayor; see above.

[2] For the valiant deeds to which Montemayor here alludes, see Menéndez Pidal, *La Leyenda del Abad Don Juan de Montemayor*, Dresden, 1903, pp. lii, and foll.

[3] Besides this, a short *cancion* which precedes, beginning " Os tempos se mudarão," and Danteo's conversation generally, are in Portuguese.

Duarda loved Danteo, who had, however, married Andresa, a shepherdess who afterwards died. Just as Felismena is about to reconcile these lovers, her attention is attracted by the voice of a combat. Upon an island in the stream she sees a knight struggling with three assailants, one of whom he kills, but the others press the knight so hard, that Felismena draws her bow and slays them. The knight turns out to be Don Felix, who is forgiven by Felismena. At this moment Dorida, the messenger of Felicia, appears with two goblets, one of silver and the other of gold, and bids Felix drink of the former, to forget his love for Celia, and of the latter, to heal his wounds.

All now return to the temple of Diana, where Felix and Felismena, Selvagia and Silvano are united and, it is presumed, live happily ever thereafter. The fate of Danteo and Duarda the author reserved for a second part.

Perhaps a few words may here be said upon the principal episodes of the *Diana*. That of the enchantress Felicia, priestess of Diana, and the magic potion she administers to the lovers to cure them of their ills, is a very old one in literature.[1] A similar incident occurs in the eighth and ninth " prosas " of the *Arcadia* of Sannazaro, and for the present purpose there is, perhaps, no need of going beyond this.

As to the story of Felix and Felismena (Book II), upon which Shakespeare is said to have founded his *Two Gentlemen of Verona,* a like expedient of a young lady disguising herself as a page to serve her lover, occurs in Bandello

---

[1] Cervantes, speaking of the *Diana,* puts these words in the mouth of the priest: " To begin, then, with the *Diana* of Montemayor. I am of the opinion it should not be burned, but that it should be cleared of all that about the sage Felicia and the magic water, and of almost all the longer pieces of verse: let it keep, and welcome, its prose and the honor of being the first of books of the kind." *Don Quixote,* I, Chap. VI.

(*Novelle*, xxxvi), first published at Lucca in 1554.[1] This novel is supposed to be the source of Shakespeare's *Twelfth Night*, and to it Giraldi Cinthio probably owes a similar story in his *Hectommithi*, printed for the first time in 1565. A like incident forms the basis of the plot of one of Lope de Rueda's best comedies, called *Comedia de los Engaños*. Indeed the plot of this comedy is very similar to the story in Bandello;[2] in both cases the twin-brother of the heroine

[1] Underhill shows that Shakespeare's version is due to the story of Montemayor, not to the novel of Bandello. He says that Shakespeare seems to have been ignorant of Spanish, nor is it probable that he had access to any English translation, unless it be Googe's eclogue. But it has long ago been pointed out by Gervinus that, in all probability, Shakespeare's source is the play called *The History of Felix and Philomena,* which was acted before the court at Greenwich on January 3, 1584. See my *Spanish Stage,* p. 77; Underhill, *Spanish Lit. in England under the Tudors,* New York, 1899, p. 363. The first trace of Montemayor's *Diana* in any other literature is found in the fifth and seventh *Eglogs* of Barnabe Googe (1563), and from the latter's very free and greatly abridged version of Felismena's story in the fifth eclogue, Shakespeare, it has been suggested, might have taken his story; but Googe's version would have given him a very imperfect idea of the story, as it omits some of its most essential features. But why could not Shakespeare have used the French translation of the *Diana* by Nicolas Colin, which appeared in 1567, and of which there were editions in 1587 and 1592? I possess the latter edition to which the other two parts have been added, translated by Gabriel Chappuys. Perhaps the critics will deny that Shakespeare had sufficient knowledge of French to read these versions. Did Shakespeare only begin his study of French in 1598, when he became a lodger in the house of Christopher Monjoy, at the corner of Silver and Monkwell Streets? For the influence of the *Diana* upon other literatures, see the excellent account of Menéndez y Pelayo, *Orígenes,* I, pp. cdlxxii ff.

[2] Klein, *Geschichte des Dramas,* Vol. IX, p. 159, has shown, however, that Bandello's novel is not the immediate source of Lope de Rueda's *Engaños,* but that the latter is merely a *rifacimento* of an Italian comedy, *Gl'Ingannati.* Dr. Horace Howard Furness is convinced that this play, *Gl'Ingannati,* composed and acted by a society or Academy named *Gl'Intronati,* at Siena in 1531, and reprinted in 1537, 1538 and

disappears in the sack of Rome by the Imperialists, and while the father and daughter, in the Italian tale, remove to Aix, in Savoy, the scene of the Spanish comedy is transferred to Modena.[1]   It is a question as to which of these two poets, Montemayor or Rueda, first introduced this story into Spanish literature.   Lope de Rueda flourished as an actor and author from about 1545 to 1565, while Montemayor wrote the *Diana* between 1554 and 1559.   Montemayor doubtless saw Rueda's plays performed in the public squares, for Rueda enjoyed great popularity throughout Spain.   However this may be, both had a source near at hand.   The same story was afterward greatly elaborated by Tirso de Molina in one of his most famous comedies, *Don Gil de las Calzas verdes.*[2]

Concerning the story of Abindarraez and Xarifa, in the fourth book of the *Diana,* there has been some discussion. It does not appear in the first edition of the *Diana* (1559 ? for it is without date), nor is it contained in the edition of Antwerp, 1561, which I possess.   According to Salvá it

1550, is the original of Bandello. He says: Apart from mere priority of date, the play itself reveals Bandello's indebtedness to it. "Shakespeare's *Twelfth Night,*" Variorum ed., Philadelphia, 1901, pp. xix, xx. Croce, *Ricerche Ispano-Italiane,* II, Naples, 1898, pp. 6 and 14, ascribes the play to A. Piccolomini, Archbishop of Patras, one of the *Intronati.* Concerning the sources of Lope de Rueda's comedies, see the very interesting article by A. L. Stiefel, in the *Zeitschrift für Roman. Phil.,* Vol. XV, pp. 183 and 318.

[1] The same plot is found in the comedia ascribed to Calderon, *La Española de Florencia.* See the article *La Española de Florencia* by Prof. Stiefel, in *Bausteine zur roman. Phil., Festgabe für Mussafia,* Halle, 1905, and the edition of the play by Dr. M. Rosenberg, Philadelphia, 1910.

[2] Schack, *Geschichte der dram. Literatur und Kunst in Spanien,* Vol. II, p. 214. *Obras de Lope Rueda* (Edicion de la Real Academia española), Madrid, 1908, Tomo I, p. lxv, of the excellent introduction by the editor, Sr. Emilio Cotarelo. Menéndez y Pelayo, *Orígenes,* I, p. cdlxviii.

was first added in the edition of Valladolid, 1561-62. Montemayor, it will be remembered, died in Feburary, 1561. Ticknor maintains that Montemayor took the story from the *Inventario* of Antonio de Villegas, of which he cites an edition of 1561.[1] For my own part I do not believe that Montemayor wrote the story that now appears in the *Diana*,[2] and agree with Ticknor that the story there printed was copied from Villégas, and amplified, despite the discrepancy in the dates. I have carefully read the two works side by side, and made many excerpts from them, where they either agreed word for word, or where the similarity was so great that it was evident one must have been

---

[1] *History of Spanish Lit.*, III, p. 95, n., and p. 153, n. Salvá, *Catálogo*, I, No. 1063, doubts the existence of this edition, the earliest known to him being Medina del Campo, 1565, though the license to print it dated 1551. It is not a question here as to the origin of this *tradicion popular*, as Gayangos calls it, the principal personage of which was an historical character, Rodrigo de Narváez, but one of priority in these two versions, of which the shortest, the simplest and the one written with most naturalness and good taste, is undoubtedly that of Villegas, and there can hardly be any doubt that the version in the *Diana* is merely an amplification of it, inserted in the work by some dishonest book-seller. Such is the opinion of Menéndez y Pelayo (*Tratado de los Romances viejos*, in *Antología de Poetas líricos Castellanos*, Tomo XII, p. 247). Sr. Menéndez, moreover, does not think that Villegas is the author of the story as it appears in his *Inventario*, but that he and the *refundidor* of the *Diana* version are equally guilty of plagiarism, the original being the very rare *Cronica del inclíto infante D. Fernando, que ganó á Antequera: en la qual trata coma se casaron á hurto el Abendarraxe (sic) Abindarraez con la linda Xarifa,* etc., a small volume in black letter which appeared s. l. n. a (probably at Zaragoza). *Ibid.,* p. 249.

[2] It is no slight satisfaction to find that this statement, made twenty years ago, has since been corroborated by no less an authority than Menéndez Pelayo (see the note above). In his *Orígenes,* I, p. cdlxviii, he says: "La historia de Abindaraez y Jarifa no es de Montemayor, y sólo después de su muerte fue interpolada in la Diana," etc. See also *ibid.,* pp. ccclxvi ff.

taken from the other.[1]   The work of Villegas is written in a very simple and graceful style, while the story in the *Diana* is prolix and verbose, is distinctly out of place, and in striking contrast with the pastoral tone of the rest of the romance.

There is no need to say anything here of the merits of the *Diana;* its beauties have been so aptly pointed out and so competently discussed, that further praise would be superfluous.[2]   It remains the best pastoral romance that Spain has produced; the tender melancholy with which it is tinged,—the reflection, doubtless, of Montemayor's own misfortunes,—lends a charm to the *Diana* that none of its imitations possess.

[1] In the *Inventario* of 1567, this story occupies leaves 94-112 in a very small octavo, while in the *Diana,* on a page containing nearly double the amount of printed matter, it occupies pages 158-180. Pages 166 and 167 of the *Diana* are almost identical, word for word, with pages 100 and 105 of the *Inventario.* See also the Spanish translation of Ticknor, III, p. 547, and Gallardo, *Ensayo,* Vol. I, No. 327, p. 357. I possess a copy of the edition of Medina del Campo, 1577, and also of a reduced fac-simile of the story of Villegas, with the title-page: *El Abencerraje de Antonio de Villegas, En Medina del Campo impresso, por Francisco del Canto. Año MDLXV.* This fac-simile, I think, is due to Sr. Asensio. Upon the story of Abindarraez in the *Diana,* Lope de Vega founded his play *El Remedio en la Desdicha.*

[2] Bouterweck, *Geschichte der Poesie und Beredsamkeit seit dem Ende des dreizehnten Jahrhunderts,* Göttingen, 1805-19, Vol. III. We may with absolute confidence accept the opinion of Menéndez y Pelayo, who says: "La *Diana* es la mejor escrita de todas las novelas pastoriles, sin exceptuar la de Gil Polo." *Orígenes,* I, p. cdlxxi.

THE "DIANA" OF ALONSO PEREZ

The *Diana* was left unfinished at Montemayor's death, the last sentence of the seventh book being: "And now all were united with those whom they loved most, to the great rejoicing of all; to which Sireno by his coming, aided not a little, although from this there followed what shall be related in the second part of this book," etc.

This 'second part' Montemayor never wrote, but in 1564 (three years after his death) Alonso Perez, a physician of Salamanca, about whose life we know nothing, published at Valencia a *Second Part of the Diana of George Montemayor.*[1] He tells us in the prologue that no one was better fitted for such a task, not because of any merit of his own, but on account of his great fondness for the writings of Montemayor. We learn, moreover, that before Montemayor left Spain he had communicated the plan of the second part of the *Diana* to Perez, which was that Delio, the husband of Diana, having died, the latter should marry Sireno, but Perez suggested that Diana remain a widow at the end of the book, and that her hand be sought by Sireno and other suitors, as this would leave the way open for a third part. To this, he says, Montemayor assented.

That the pedantic physician had no small opinion of his own ability is evident, for he observes that Montemayor would have been better equipped for his task had he possessed a knowledge of Latin. This of course Perez had

---

[1] According to Nicolas Antonio, it also appeared at Alcalá in the same year.

and he proudly bids the reader observe that there is scarcely any thing in his book, whether prose or verse, that has not, in part at least, been stolen or imitated from the Italian or Latin writers, nor does he think that any blame attaches to him on this account, " because they did the same with the Greeks." We do not expect much after this candid confession, nor are we disappointed. Menéndez y Pelayo remarks that the most casual inspection of the volume,—for to read it entirely is almost impossible,—shows that Sannazaro's *Arcadia* and Ovid's *Metamorphoses* and *Fasti* are the principal authors sacked by the physician.[1] The main incidents of this ' Second Part ' are subjoined:

A number of shepherds and shepherdesses visit the temple of Diana, " where the wise Felicia dwells." . . . " And not many days after, Felicia one night after supper saide thus to Sylvanus and Selvagia:[2] I could not choose but blame you fortunate shepherds for the small care you have of your flockes, if I myselfe were not in fault, because you have never asked after them in all this time, nor (I thinke) once remembered them, fearing lest by reason of your absence, they have been in great want, and not without cause, being not carried to feed at convenient times upon the

[1] *Orígenes,* I, p. cdlxxix.

[2] The English in quotation marks is taken from the translation by Bartholomew Yong, which embraces the three parts of the *Diana,* Montemayor's original, and the continuations by Alonso Perez and Gaspar Gil Polo. Though finished in 1583, Yong first printed his *Diana* in London, in 1598. He seems to have passed nearly three years in Spain, returning in 1579. His translation of the prose portions of the *Diana* is very faithful to the original—his rendering of the verse, however, is very unfortunate. In 1596 Thomas Wilson finished his translation of the *Diana,* which is now in the British Museum: Ms. Add. 18638. It is entitled: *Diana de Monte mayor done out of Spanish by Thomas Wilson, Esquire. In the yeare 1596 & dedicated to the Erle of Southampton who was then uppon ye Spanish voiage wth my Lord of Essex.* I purpose publishing this soon.

greene and sauorie grasse nor (at their neede) driven to the cleere springs to quench their burning thirst, nor with wonted loue put into the coole and pleasant shades." Felicia now bids Sylvanus and Selvagia depart, whereupon Sylvanus "made louing signes to Seluagia to answer the ladies intent. To whom, with a seemly blush, as partly ashamed thereat, she saide in this sort. It is now no time (my deere Sylvanus) to use circumstances of such arte, where there is no cause, neither doe they well become this place. For though their usage to all women is commendable, yet not in particular, for the husband to his wife, and in such sort as if he went about to preferre her before himselfe. For after that the woman hath delivered herself into the possession of her husband, she therewithal yieldeth up to his jurisdiction the title of her libertie, by the sweete and sacred bond of marriage." Syrenus, another shepherd, sings and Sylvanus responds. All now retire to resume their way on the next morning. "Felicia gave Dorida in charge to fill their scrips the night before, with sufficient provisions for their way, who like a friendly and louing nymph, that was not slacke to serve their necessitie (que no los queria mal), going about it immediately, did put into the same good store of victuals."

They now observe a shepherd coming along, singing the following sonnet:

> De donde, o papel mio, tal ventura,
>   Que sin meritos ayas de ser puesto
>   Delante el resplandor, y claro gesto,
>   En el qual su poder mostra natura.
> Verás papel amado la figura
>   Do no ay mas que esperar del ser honesto,
>   Verás sumado en breue todo el resto
>   De gracia, gallardia, y hermosura.
> En viendote ante aquesta mi pastora,
>   Dirásle de mi parte: Acà me embia
>   Quien viue por seruiros tanto tiempo!

En este solo entiende qualquier hora,
   en esto se desuela noche, y dia,
   Seruiros es su solo pasatiempo.[1]

The shepherds now sitting down by a stream, Syrenus says: " Is it not reason Sylvanus, that living now in such joy and content, and in the presence of thy beloved Selvagia, thou shouldst let thy Bagpipe wax to drie? Sylvanus sings:

Podra verse yr el cielo con sossiego,
Y aun por algun espacio detenerse,
Y las aguas de Ezla y de Mondego
Con passo apressurado atras boluerse;
Y puestas á la llama de un gran fuego,
La estopa y seca caña no encenderse,
Mas no se verá un dia, ni una hora
Dexar de amar Sylvano á su pastora.[2]

---

[1] From whence, O paper mine, such happy favour
That undeservedly thou must be placed
Before that flower that yields the sweetest savour,
Which nature hath with all her powers graced?
Thou shalt the figure see (my louing paper)
Where all the virtues make their wished dwelling,
And of the rest not any one escape her,
Graces and giftes and beauties most excelling.
Then when thou com'st before my heauenly treasure
Say thus from me to her. He sends me hither
Who lives to serve thee while his life extendeth:
In only this his thoughts are musing ever:
In joy of this both nights and days he spendeth;
To serve thee is his only sport and pleasure.
                       Yong's translation.

[2] It may fall out the heavens may turn at leisure,
And stay themselves upon the highest mountaines;
And Ezla and Mondego at their pleasure
With hastie course turne back unto their fountaines:
And that the flaxe or reede, laid to the fire,
May not consume in flames but burn like wire;
But yet the day and time shall happen never
When Sylvan shall not love Seluagia ever.

" Immediately, without any entreatie, Seluagia, because
she would not die in Sylvanus' debt (por no dever cosa a
su Sylvano), nor be beholding to him in this respect, taking
her Baggepipe up, in this sort did answer him:

> La tierra dexara de ser pisada,
> Su natural y proprio ser perdiendo;
> El agua podra ser menospreciada,
> De plantas humedad ya no teniendo.
> Nuestra vida podra ser sustentada
> Sin ayre para ella no siruiendo,
> Mas no verá jamas algun humano
> Dexar de amar Selvagia á su Sylvano.[1]

And thus do these good shepherds swear eternal constancy in continually exaggerated phrase, until the limit of
the Spanish language is reached, when they rise and " casting their heauy scrippes on their shoulders, staying them-
selues upon their knotty sheepehookes," they continue
their way, reaching their own fields the next day, where
they see Diana " standing very sadde and leaning against
a great Oke, with her elbow upon her sheepehooke and her
cheeke upon the palm of her hande, whereby one might
haue iudged the care and sorrow that so much troubled
her pensive minde." " After a while (as though she was
angry with herselfe for casting herselfe into so great a
greefe) she put her hand into her bosom, and tooke out a
fine little baggepipe, and which putting to her mouth to
play on it, in that very instant, she threw it to the ground,
and without more adoe, sliding down along the bodie of the

---

[1] The ground shall first be void, nor trod nor usèd,
Losing her nature, and her proper being;
First shall the raine and water be refusèd
Of plants no moisture round about them seeing:
First shall our life with air be not sustainèd,
And first the food of hunger be distainèd,
Before the world shall see a deede so hainous,
Seluagia not to loue her deere Sylvanus.

tree, sat her downe, as if for great feeblenes she had not been able to staie herself on her feete, and casting out a sorrowful sigh, and looking upon her harmlesse Baggepipe, she spake these words: Accursed Baggepipe," etc. The shepherds console Diana, who now departs. She is pursued by Firmius, a shepherd who had been standing behind a convenient tree, escapes, however, and Firmius returns. They all continue their way and approach the town, where they meet a number of shepherds and shepherdesses, among them Diana, who requests Firmius to sing, to which he replies: " I will sing, though it be with a hoarce voice like to the dying swanne divining her ensuing death." " Thou are not so neere thy end (saide Diana) that death should helpe thee." " I am so neere ended (saide Firmius) that I looke only but for death." " I did never yet see any (saide Diana) die for this cause, but with wordes, and do believe besides, there are not any such." (A nadie he visto, dixo Diana, sino es de palabra morir, ni lo creo.) The next day all departed for Felicia's palace.

At sunset they come to an island which they had before visited, and here they find Felicia and her nymphs, with Don Felix and Felismena. An old man appears, " in every point he seemed to represent a most woorthie priest of Jupiter," who rails against fortune in good set terms to the extent of six stanzas. It is Parisiles, whose long lost daughter Stela is now restored to him. She appears with Crimine and a young shepherd, " a goodly youth of person; his weedes were of gray cloth (pardo) to signify by that colour his troubles and griefs. All along the boarder of his coate sleeves went three ribbons or laces of sundry colours, two of them on either side, of lion tawney and olive green (aceitunador), to signify by the first his sorrow and by the second his torment." The young shepherd, Delicius, relates a long and tedious story of his like-

ness to Parthenio and the rescue of Stela. They now re-
pair to Felicia's palace, over the principal gate of which
they see two nymphs of silver upon the capitals of the columns and the verses:

> Quien entra, mire bien como ha viuido
> Y el don de castidad si l'ha guardado,
> Y la que quiere bien, o l'ha querido,
> Mire si á causa de otra s'ha mudado;
> Y si la fe primera no ha perdido,
> Y aquel primor amor ha conseruado,
> Entrar puede en el templo de Diana
> Cuya virtud y gracia es sobr' humana.[1]
>
> (Book III, fol. 86.)

Felicia now accompanies her guests to the fountain of
the Laurel trees, where " they sawe two lovely shepherdesses (though by their coye looks shewing a kind of sig-
norie and statelinesse above any other) that were sitting
harde by the goodly spring, both of them endowed with
singular beautie, but especially the one, that to their iudge-
ment seemed the yoonger. Right over against them on
foote stoode a young shepherd, who with the lappe of his
side coate wiped away the teares that fell down thicke upon
his blubbered cheekes (limpeandose con la faldilla del sayo
las lagrimas que por su rostro decendian), in requital
whereof, and of his inwarde greefe, the shepherdesses did
nothing else but by looking upon one another, affoord him

---

[1] This inscription is taken from Book IV of the *Diana* of Montemayor:

> Who comes into this palace let her take heede
> How she hath liv'd, and whether she hath kept
> The gift of chastitie in thought and deede.
> And see besides, if she hath ever stept,
> With wavering mind to forren love estranged,
> And for the same her first affection changed,
> May enter in Diana's Temple heere,
> Whose grace and virtues soveraine appear.

a gracious smile." The shepherd, after singing " with his
many teeres " takes his leave, whereupon Phillis, " being
mooved to some small sorrow and to no lesse greefe for his
departure, took out of her scrip a fine little spoone (the
same perhaps that she herselfe did eat with) and gave it
him, wherewith the shepherd did somewhat mitigate his
helplesse sorrow." Crimine being requested to tell her
story says: " Alas! who can quench my scalding sighes,
that with such a heauie recital will come smoking out of
my baleful breast? " (Ay de mi, quien podra amatar mis
encendidos suspiros, que con tal memoria de mis ojos, y
entrañas saldran.) Continuing, she says: " you must understand that I love the shepherd that is our guide in our
travels (Delicio), as much as I can and can in truth as
much as I will. I love also Parthenio his friend as much as
I will and will truly as much as I can; [1] for as it cannot be
discerned which is Delicio and which Parthenio, and the
one impossible to be knowen from the other, for like two
drops of water they resemble one another so much; so
cannot I tell, which of them I love most, loving both in
equal balance of extreme affection." Delicio and Parthenio
now explain that the object of their pilgrimage is to seek
out their fathers, " with certaine tokens that we carry with
us to know them," for as little children they had been
given away to be brought up. They resolve to remain for
a while. " The next day going very softly about the same
hower, and by secret places to see how the shepherds were
occupied, we found them sitting upon the greene grass,
and sleeping in such sort, that they shewed that that was
not their principall intent; for the christalline teares, that

---

[1] " Entended que yo amo a este pastor que con nosotros viene
quanto puedo, y puedo a la verdad quanto quiero. Amo assi mismo
a Parthenio amigo suyo, quanto quiero, y quiero cierto quanto puedo "
(p. 497).

trickled down their burning cheekes in corriualtie, signified more store of sorrowful thoughts in their harts, then heauy vapours in their heads." [1]

Parthenio finds some verses on the bark of a tree; there are fifteen stanzas in all; here is the last:

> Porque de tal modo ofende
> al coraçon hecho fragua,
> que muy crece y s'estiende,
> y muy mucho mas s'enciende
> quanto mas se le echa d'agua.
> Pues ya me falta la haya,
> no faltandome el penar,
> bien sera que no me vaya
> a buscar tronco en que caya
> lo que aqui no puede estar." [2]
>
> (Book IV, fol. 116.)

Don Felix now inquires about the poem on the tree and bids Crimine recite it, but Doria said: " I would first know if it be such a one as the last, for if it be not, she did well to leauue off her tale at such a point; for it is not the condition of my palate to remain with an ill taste, when it hath once a good one " (porque no es de mi paladar, quedar con mal gusto, si puede tenerle bueno).

---

[1] " Y de tal manera durmiendo, que mostrauan no ser aquel su principal intento; porque las cristalinas lagrimas que por sus encendidas mexillas en cōpetencia decendian, significauan auer mas abundancia de cōgoxosos pensamientos en el coraçon, que cantidad de soporiferos vapores en el celebro' (p. 507).

[2] And in such sort, because it doth offend
My heart that burns like to the smithie flame
For it doth more increase and doth extend,
And more it doth with sparkling flames incend,
The more that water's cast upon the same:
And now since want of hedgerow faileth me,
And that I feele increase, not want of paine,
I think it best for me to goe and see
If I can finde some other hedge or tree,
To write that there, which this cannot containe.

The trees, however, are full of poetry, for the next day they find a sycamore, on the bark of which is a poem in fourteen stanzas of ten lines each. Sitting beneath the trees the shepherds indulge in long conversations " in all which time neither Rebecke nor Baggepipe were heard, unless it were when other nymphs came: for when louers are alone, singing (I thinke) and musicke pleaseth not their musing mindes so much as the mutuall contemplation and looking of one another; and that talking and amorous conversation should be more pleasant and sweete to them, then the melodie of sweete musicke." [1] That evening they sat beneath "a leafie sallow tree," when fierce Gorphorost, a giant from whose pursuit Stela saved herself by leaping into a stream, came out of his cave and approached the spot where Stela had cast herself into the river. " After he had sit down a little while and laid his scrip by his side, he took a flute out of it, made of a hundred Baggepipes joined together with waxe. Putting it to his mouth and blowing it strongly to cleere it of filth within (puesta a la boca y tocada con furia para limpiarla, si alguna suziedad tenia dentro), the hills resounded againe, the rivers ranne backe, the wilde beasts and fish were stroken in a feare and the forrests and woods thereabouts began to tremble." Being a lusty giant, he sings twenty-six stanzas, then seizes one of his rivals, Parthenio, believing that he is Delicio, and casts him into a cave. Stela and Crimena in their search for him, meet a shepherdess, who, flinging a ball into the air, runs away. On picking up the ball they find that it is made of linen, upon which Parthenio has written a note. How Parthenio returns we are not told, but we find him

---

[1] " Creo yo que estando solos los que bien se aman, que no ay cantar, ni tañer, sino contemplar, y hablar, deue de ser mas apazible la conversacion de amorosas palabras que la melodia de la dulce musica" (p. 546).

safe and sound in the next book, which opens with a
thunder storm. A shepherd arrives, who is seeking a place
to sleep, for he says " they tell me that lightning spares
those who sleep." [1]

He is the only happy shepherd that has yet appeared, and
rejoices

> " de ser el mas felice que ha nacido
> entre aquellos que sirven a Cupido."

He bids all the shepherds leave their lasses and come to
love his:

> " dexad vuestras zagales al instante
> venid a amar a esta mi pastora."

Alas! it is no longer time, Sylvanus saying: " By my
faith, friend shepherd, thou commest too late with thy
counsell. For to leaue of that which we have already for
this yoong shepherdesse, I thinke there is no remedie."
The new comer tells of a famous shepherd in the country
of St. Stephen, who came there from foreign lands, to
whose great knowledge nature herself seemed subject. " O
what great profit do we and our flockes receive by his companie with us! We, by easing us of our continuall labours
by his industry; our flockes by healing their common dis-
eases. If there were any gadding goat that estraying from
his companie, did put us to trouble in seeking him, by
cutting his beard, he made him keep still with the flock.
If the Ram, which for guide of the rest we chose out for
the stoutest, we could not make gentle, be made more mild
then a lamb, by making holes thorow his hornes hard by
his eares. He told us the fuls and wanes of the Moone,
by the Antes and the dores (escarabajos = beetles). For

---

[1] " Porque me dizen que perdona el rayo a los que duermen."

the Antes betweene the Moones take their rest, and in the full labour night and day." [1]　He also tells of the love of Firmius and Faustus for Diana, and presently Diana disappears with Faustus, when, however, another shepherdess, Cardenia, appears.　She complains that Faustus " did once love her," and weeping, wipes away her tears, " con una cristalina mano, que no en pequeña admiracion puso a los pastores, que la vieron."　She now recites the sonnets and letters Faustus had sent her, saying: " To any of these I never had an answer, whereupon I thinke he never made account of them, and of the last especially, because he had quite forgotten me when that came."　A shepherd is heard singing:

> " Guardame mis vacas
> Carillo, por tu fé,
> Besame primero
> Y te las guardaré."

They depart again for Felicia's palace, whither come also " a pilgrim called Placindus, and Danteus and Duarda, the portingall shepherdess."

Placindas now relates the story of Disteus, " descended from the race of King Eolus in Eolia, whom they afterwards called the God of the winds, and of his love for Dardanea, sister of Sagastes."　The story is long drawn out, the result being that Delicio and Parthenio are the sons of Disteus and Dardanea, who flee to Trinacria, where the former becomes a shepherd " to dissemble his noble condition with his base estate."

In the last two books sight is lost entirely of Diana, who is now a widow, Delio, her husband, having died, we are told.　At the conclusion the author says: " whoever desires

---

[1] " Porque las hormigas entre lunas reposan, y en el lleno, aun todas las noches trabajan."

to see the obsequies of Delio, the rivalry of Faustus, Firmio and Sireno, etc., let him attend me in the third part of this work, which shall soon be printed, God willing. It was not added here not to make too large a volume." [1]

The inferiority of this continuation to the original of Montemayor is at once apparent, nor did it at any time meet with much success. Salvá gives no separate edition of the work of Perez after the first one of 1564 at Alcalá de Henares. In every respect it falls below the *Diana;* it does not maintain its moral standard; a host of new characters is brought upon the scene, who appear and disappear without any motive, serving only to complicate the narrative and confuse the reader; the various incidents are clumsily introduced, showing an entire lack of invention, and contribute nothing to advance the main story, the thread of which is, in fact, entirely lost in the seventh and eighth books, leaving us in complete ignorance of the fate of the principal characters, which is to be disclosed, according to the author's promise, in a part which never appeared. In short, the prose of the *Diana* of Perez is prolix and tedious, and its poetry never rises above mediocrity.

[1] See the criticism of the curate, in the examination of Don Quixote's library. Part I, Chap. vi. It would seem from the above that the 'third part' was already written.

THE "DIANA ENAMORADA" OF GIL POLO.

In the same year, 1654, there appeared at Valencia the *Diana enamorada,* of Gaspar Gil Polo, likewise a continuation of Montemayor's *Diana.*[1] Polo was a native of Valencia; not the professor of Greek in the University of that city, as Ticknor says, nor the "elegante jurisconsulto," given as the author by Nicolas Antonio, Rodriguez and Ximeno, but the father of the great jurist, as Fuster, it seems to me, has conclusively shown.[2]

[1] *Primera parte de Diana enamorada, cinco libros que prosiguen los siete de la Diana de Jorge de Montemayor, compuestos por Gaspar Gil Polo: dirigidos a la muy Ilustre Señora Doña Hieronima de Castro y Bolea.—Con Privilegio en Valencia en casa de Joan Mey, año de 1564.*
The following letter, omitted in the only version accessible to me, is interesting: *A los lectores.*—. . . Puse aqui algunas *rimas y versos de estilo nuevo,* y hasta agora (que yo sepa), no usado en esta lengua. Las *Rimas* hice a imitacion de las que he leido en libros antiguos de Poetas Provenzales, y por eso les dí este nombre. Los versos compuse a semejanza de los que en lengua francesa llaman *heróicos,* y ansi los nombré *franceses:* díle la *rima* que por agora me paresció mejor. Quien dello se contentare, podrá probar la mano a hacer dellos *tercetos* y otras *rimas,* que no dejaran de parescer muy bien. A este libro nombré *Diana enamorada,* porque prosiguiendo la Diana de Montemayor, me paresció convenirle este nombre, pues él dejó a la pastora en este trance. El que tuvíere por deshonesto el nombre de *enamorada,* no me condene hasta ver la honestidad que aqui se trata, el decoro que se guarda en la persona de Diana. . . . Hallareis aqui proseguidas y rematadas las historias que Jorge de Montemayor dejó por acabar, y muchas añadidas." Gallardo, *Ensayo,* III, col. 1242. This edition was followed by one at Antwerp, 1567. See Salvá, *Catálogo,* II, p. 145.

[2] Fuster, *Biblioteca Valenciana,* Tome I, p. 150, *et seq.* It is unnecessary to quote his arguments at length. He shows that Dr. Gaspar Gil Polo, to whom the above writers attribute the *Diana enamorada,* was the son of Gaspar Gil Polo and Isabel Gil; that he was an

Polo's work is vastly superior to that of Perez, and was received with great public favor. It was highly praised by Cervantes, and Nicolas Antonio even said: *vel aequavit Georgium, vel superavit.*[1]

The *Diana enamorada* opens with the recovery of Sireno from the influence of the draught administered by Felicia, and as a result of which he becomes entirely indifferent to Diana, who complains of his neglect. She visits the " fountain of the Alders," besides which she had so often sat in the company of Sireno, and while bewailing her lot,[2] is

advocate of the 'Brazo Real' at the Cortes held at Monzon in 1626. As the *Diana* of Polo first appeared in 1564, supposing him to have written it when twenty years old, he must have been eighty-two years old in 1626, an age, he shows, at which he could not have performed the duties devolving upon his office. Other evidence is adduced to prove that in 1564 Dr. Polo was not more than sixteen or seventeen years of age. His conclusion is that the author of the *Diana enamorada* was Gaspar Gil Polo, the father of Dr. Polo, the jurist, as he was the only other member of that family in Valencia, who, in addition to *Gaspar,* bore the name *Gil.* The name of the Greek professor at Valencia from 1566 to 1574 was simply Gil Polo. Fuster gives a sonnet by our author, prefixed to *La Pasion de Nuestro Señor Jesucristo,* by D. Alonso Giron y Rebolledo, published at Valencia in 1563. Rebolledo wrote a complimentary sonnet to the *Diana enamorada.*

[1] The *Diana* of Perez, 'the Salamancan,' which we have just noticed, is, on the contrary, incontinently committed to the heap of rubbish in the yard. "Este que sigue, dejó el Barbero, es *La Diana,* llamada *Segunda del Salmantino:* y este, otro que tiene el mismo nombre, cuyo autor es Gil Polo. Pues la del Salmantino, respondió el Cura, acompañe y acreciente el numero de los condenados al corral, y la de Gil Polo se guarde como si fuera del mismo Apolo." *Don Quixote,* Part I, Chap. vi. It is possible that the pun upon *Polo* and *Apolo* may, in some measure, be responsible for this high estimate of our author. However, Cervantes also praises Polo in his *Canto de Caliope* in his *Galatea,* Book vi.

[2] Diana sings:

> " Mi sufrimiento cansado
> del mal importuno y fiero
> a tal estremo ha llegado,
> que publicar mi cuydado

overheard by a shepherd who has been listening in the bushes, and, who now advancing, requests Diana to relate the story of her life, with which the latter, fascinated by the beauty of the shepherdess, complies, cautioning the stranger, however, to be content to know her name, but not her sufferings. The shepherdess (Alcida) replies: " I know very well, from the story I have just heard you sing. that your grief is love, in which infirmity I have great experience. Many years have I been a slave, but now I am free; I walked blindly, but now I tread the paths of truth. Upon the sea of love I endured frightful agonies and torments, but now I enjoy a safe and calm haven."

A long discussion follows, in which Alcida maintains that love exists only in the imagination, and that its power is due only to the fact that no resistance is ever offered to it. She recites the following sonnet:

No es ciego Amor, mas yo lo soy, que guio
mi voluntad camino del tormento:
no es niño Amor: mas yo que en un momento
espero y tengo miedo, lloro y rio.

Nombrar llamas de Amor es desvario,
su fuego es el ardiente y vivo intento,
sus alas son mi altivo pensamiento,
y la esperanza vana en que me fio.

No tiene Amor cadenas, ni saëtas,
para prender y herir libres y sanos,
que en él no hay mas poder del que le damos.

Porque es Amor mentira de poetas,
sueño de locos, idolo de vanos;
mirad qué negro Dios el que adoramos.[1]

me es el remedio postrero.
Sientase el bravo dolor
y trabajosa agonia
de la que muere de amor,
y olvidada de un pastor,
que de olvidado moria," etc.

[1] Loue is not blinde, but I, which fondly guide
My will to tread the path of amorous paine:

She continues to rail against love, adding: " all the verses of lovers are full of grief, composed with sighs, blotted with tears and sung with agony." Hardly had Alcida spoken these words when Diana perceived far off her husband, Delio,[1] saying: " Behold my Delio! We must dissemble what we have been discussing. Whereupon they sing some *Rimas provenzales*. The jealous Delio approaches and is received by his wife " with an angelic countenance." Delio, of course, becomes desperately enamoured of Alcida. A voice is now heard, " the sweetness of which delights them marvelously," and presently they see a "weary shepherd" approaching the fountain. He is singing, the concluding lines of his song being:

> "Love, why dost thou not loose my chains,
>   Since in such liberty thou hast left Alcida."

Alcida, immediately recognizing the voice as Marcelio's, bids Diana not to betray her presence, and hastens away through a thick wood to escape this shepherd, " whom she abhorred like death itself." Marcelio arrives " so weary and distressed that it seemed that fortune was grieving at having offered him that clear fountain and the company of

> Loue is no childe, but I, which all in vaine,
> Hope, fear, and laugh, and weepe on euery side:
> Madness to say, that flames are Cupid's pride,
> For my desire his fier doth containe,
> His wings my thoughts most high and soueraine,
> And that vaine hope, wherein my ioies abide:
> Loue hath no chaines, nor shaftes of such intent,
> To take and wound the whole and freest minde
> Whose power (then we giue him) is no more,
> For loue's a tale, that poets did inuent,
> A dreame of fooles, and idoll vain and blinde:
> See then how black a God doe we adore?
>   —Yong's translation.

[1] Delio, it will be remembered, was dead at the conclusion of the second part of the *Diana* of Perez.

Diana, as some relief to his sufferings" ("tan cansado y afligido, que paresció la fortuna doliendose dél, havelle ofrescido aquella clara fuente, y la compañia de Diana para algun alivio de su pena"). Delio now pursues Alcida, and is deaf to the call of Diana, while the newly-arrived Marcelio is seeking Alcida. Marcelio, at Diana's request, now recites the story of his life; that he lived at the court of Portugal, entered the army in Africa, where he was betrothed to Alcida, daughter of a distinguished knight, Eugerio; of his shipwreck while on his way to Lisbon to celebrate the nuptials; of the treachery of the sailors who carried off Clenarda, the sister of Alcida, and separated him from Alcida, and how finally he was rescued by fishermen, and of his vain search for Alcida ever since. "Marcelio now began to weep so bitterly and to sigh so dolorously, that it was a great pity to see him."

Diana, however, knowing that even a love-lorn shepherd needs something more substantial than tears and sighs, says: "Since I am forsaken by my husband Delio, as you are by Alcida, suppose we eat a few bites together." And they eat. Two shepherds, Tauriso and Berardo, "que por Diana penados andaban," now appear and sing of Diana. Some of these verses are clearly reminiscent of Garcilaso:

> "Un dia al campo vino,
> Aserenado el cielo,
> La luz de perfectissimas mugeres,
> Las hebras de oro fino
> Cubiertas con un velo,
> Prendido con dorados alfileres;
> Mil juegos y placeres
> Passaba con su esposo,
> Yo tras un myrtho estaba,
> Y vi que él alargaba
> La mano al blanco velo, y el hermoso
> Cabello quedó suelto,
> Y yo de vello en triste miedo envuelto."

All now resolve to visit the Temple of Diana on the morrow. Accordingly the next morning, when " la rubicunda Aurora con su dorado gesto ahuyentaba las nocturnas estrellas, y las aves con suave canto anunciaban el cercano dia, la enamorada Diana," with her bagpipe and her scrip filled with provisions, sets forth. She is, however, too early for the weary Marcelio, and while sitting down to wait for him, she sings a *cancion,* beginning:

" Madruga un poco, luz del claro dia,

and ending:

Cancion, en algun pino, o dura encina
No quise señalarte,
Mas antes entregarte
Al sordo campo y al mudable viento;
Porque de mi tormento
Se pierda la noticea y la memoria,
Pues ya perdida está mi vida y gloria.   (Book II.)

Soon the ' desamado ' Marcelio appears, and like a well-bred shepherd, apologizes for his tardiness. Diana now relates that she has been forsaken by Sireno, " by whom she was formerly loved," but fate, " which perverts all human intentions," willed that she should obey her father and marry the jealous Delio. A long discussion now follows on jealousy,—its nature and causes. Presently they enter a delightful little grove and hear a plaintive voice accompanied by a sweet lyre, singing a strange melody." " After this shepherdess had ceased her sweet singing, loosing the reins to bitter and grievous weeping, she shed such an abundance of tears and uttered such sad groans, that by them and the words she spake, we knew that the cause of her grief was some cruel deception of her suspicious husband." Diana and Marcelio approach the shepherdess, who says: " Since I was forsaken by my cruel spouse, I do not remember to have experienced so much joy as I now do to see you." The strange shepherdess is Ismenia, in love with Montano. She is, however, also beloved by Fileno, Montano's father,—hence all her troubles. She relates how the "enamorado viejo" promised her many jewels and dresses and sent her many letters. In one of them he says: "I know very well that I am old, but old age has its advantages, for human habitations, however modern, are not to be compared with those of the ancient Romans, and in matters of beauty, splendor and gallantry, the saying is, there is nothing like the past." [1]

Ismenia finally married Montano, incurring the wrath of Fileno,—who now marries Felisarda, whom Montano formerly loved but had rejected, and who now conspires with a shepherdess named Sylveria, to ruin Montano. The plan is not successful, but Montano's jealousy being aroused by some remarks his father had made, he leaves the village. never to return. Since that time Ismenia has sought Montano, to free herself of the stain upon her. On concluding her story, they betake themselves to a delightful forest, where they hear the songs of shepherds, who, as they learn afterwards, are Tauriso and Berardo. While listening to the songs of the shepherds they hear the voices of a man and a woman, who are found to be Polydoro and Clenarda, the brother and sister of Alcida. There is great rejoicing, after which they sit by the fountain and eat, and during the repast Polydoro relates how he escaped, with his father,

[1] "Los edificios humanos
quanto mas modernos son,
no tienen comparacion
con los antiguos Romanos.
Y en las cosas de primor,
gala, asseo y valentia,
suelen decir cada dia,
lo passado es lo mejor."

from the shipwreck, and how they were rescued on the coast of Valencia by fishermen,[1] who tell them that on that same morning they had also rescued a woman from a distressed vessel, and repairing to the hut of the fishermen, they find Clenarda, singing with the fisherman's daughters, one of whom, named Nerea, now sings a *cancion.*[2]

[1] One of the sailors sings the following sonnet:

> Recoge a los que aflige el mar ayrado,
> ¡O Valentino! O venturoso suelo!
> Donde jamás se quaja el duro hielo,
> Ni da Phebo el trabajo acostumbrado.
>
> Dichoso el que seguro y sin recelo
> De ser en fieras ondas anegado,
> Goza de la belleza de tu prado,
> Y del favor de tu benigno cielo.
>
> Con mas fatiga el mar sulca la nave,
> Que el labrador cansado tus barvechos;
> ¡O tierra! antes que el mar se ensobervezca,
> Recoge á los perdidos y deshechos,
> Para que quando en Turia yo me lave,
> Estas malditas aguas aborrezca.

[2] This *Cancion de Nerea* is very beautiful. In the following stanzas Sr. Menéndez Pelayo detects an imitation of Virgil's ninth Eclogue, the lines beginning: Huc ades, o Galatea, quis est nam ludus in undis? etc.:

> Nympha hermosa, no te vea
> Jugar con el mar horrendo,
> Y aunque mas placer te sea,
> Huye del mar, Galatea,
> Como estás de Lycio huyendo.
> *   *   *   *   *   *
>
> Ven comigo al bosque ameno
> Y al apacible sombrio
> De olorosas flores lleno,
> Do en el dia mas sereno
> No es enojoso el Estio. . . .
> *   *   *   *   *   *
>
> Huye los sobervios mares,
> Ven, veras como cantamos
> Tan deleytosos cantares,
> Que los mas duros pesares
> Suspendemos y engañamos. . . .   (Book III.)

At the conclusion of Polydoro's story, Clenarda recites her adventures, and the next day they go to the Temple of Diana, where the sage Felicia dwells, who would alleviate all their woes. Here they find Syreno. As a pastime during their wanderings, Clenarda tells of her adventures in the fields and along the banks of the Guadalquivir, and what she had heard of the famous Turia, the principal river of that land. One day Polydoro and Clenarda, arriving at the hut of a cowherd, were told that they should not fail to hear the legend which the famous *Turia* would shortly sing. They proceed to a spacious meadow, where they saw a great number of nymphs and shepherds, all waiting for the famous *Turia* to begin his song. " Not long after this, we saw old *Turia* come out of a deep cave, in his hand an urn or vase, very large and ornamental, his head covered with leaves of oak and laurel, his arms hairy, his beard slimy and gray. . . ." " And sitting upon the ground, reclining upon the urn and pouring forth from it an abundance of clear water, raising his hoarse voice, he sang the celebrated *Canto de Turia,* in praise of the Valencian poets."

A beautiful nymph, Arethusa, who had been gathering flowers, now conducts them to the temple. Diana asks her: " What is there now in these parts?" Arethusa replies: " What is newest hereabouts is that two hours ago a lady dressed as a shepherdess, arrived at the house of Felicia, who, being seen by an old man present, was recognized as his daughter. The name of the old man, if I remember rightly, is Eugerio, and that of the daughter, Alcida." Among the other shepherds and shepherdesses present are Sylvano and Selvagia, Arsileo and Belisa, " and the chief one, called Syreno:" Felicia receives them graciously; all is explained satisfactorily between Clenarda and Alcida, and they retire, to meet at the fountain next morning.

" Then, as the expectation of such pleasure made them all pass the night with difficulty, " they all arose so early that long before the hour agreed upon they arrived at the fountain with their instruments, " and began to sing and play by the light of the moon." Diana and Ismenia were still sleeping, however, but being awakened by footsteps, Ismenia rouses Diana, who, knocking on the wall, wakes Marcelio. Ismenia now hears someone singing a *Sextine,* and at once recognizes the voice as that of her husband, Montano. Presently Diana also hears the voice of Syreno. They go to the garden to await Felicia, where Marcelio sees Don Felix and Felismena, " marido y muger," to whom he is presented by Sylvano, whom he meets there with Selvagia. Marcelio now discovers that Felismena is his sister. Alcida relates how Delio followed her, " and when all hope was gone," grew ill, and was nursed by a shepherd, who sent for Delio's mother. The latter " asked him the cause of his grief, but he gave no reply and only wept and sighed," and finally " con un desmayo acabó la vida con mucho dolor de su triste madre, parientos y amigos." And now Marcelio and Alcida, and Diana and Syreno are happily united by the " sapientissima " Felicia, Arsileo singing some *versos franceses* in honor of the marriage.[1]

---

[1] These *versos franceses,* which are considered among the most beautiful poetry in the *Diana enamorada,* and, in the opinion of Menéndez y Pelayo (*Orígenes,* I. p. cdlxxxviii) perhaps the only alexandrines composed in Spain in the sixteenth century, are as follows:

> De flores matizadas se vista el verde prado,
> Retumbe el hueco bosque de voces deleitosas,
> Olor tengan mas fino las coloradas rosas,
> Floridos ramos mueva el viento sossegado.
> El rio apressurado
> Sus aguas acresciente,
> Y pues tan libre queda la fatigada gente

The fifth book consists merely of the festivities in the garden of Felicia, " to celebrate the marriages and ' desengaños ' of the shepherds." Diana sings a *cancion:*

> " La alma de alegría salte,
> Que en tener mi bien presente
> No hay descanso que me falte,
> Ni dolor que me atormente.
>
> No pienso en viejos cuidados,
> Que agravia muestros amores
> Tener presentes dolores
> Por los olvidos pasados.
> Alma, de tu dicha valte,
> Que con bien tan excelente
> No hay descanso que te falte,
> Ni dolor que te atormente."

While Diana is singing, Melisea, another love-lorn shepherdess, appears, followed by Narciso, who comes to seek

> Del congojoso llanto,
> Moved, hermosas Nymphas, regocijado canto.
> *   *   *   *   *   *   *
> Casados venturosos, el poderoso cielo
> Derrame en vuestros campos influxo favorable,
> Y con dobladas crias en numero admirable
> Vuestros ganados crezcan cubriendo el ancho suelo.
> No os dañe el crudo hielo
> Los tiernos chivaticos,
> Y tal cantidad de oro os haga entrambos ricos,
> Que no sepais el quanto:
> Moved, hermosas Nymphas, regocijado canto.
> *   *   *   *   *   *   *
> Remeden vuestras voces las aves amorosas,
> Los ventecicos suaves os hagan dulce fiesta,
> Alegrese con veros el campo y la floresta,
> Y os vengan a las manos las flores olorosas:
> Los lirios y las rosas,
> Jazmin y flor de Gnido,
> La madreselva hermosa y el arrayan florido,
> Narciso y amaranto:
> Moved, hermosas Nymphas, regocijado canto.   (Book IV.)

the aid of Felicia. And now Ismenia, " her face giving signs of the inward happiness she feels after such protracted cares," sings another cancion. After a dance by a troupe of nymphs around " a white stag with black spots," the symbolical meaning of which is explained by Felicia, the whole company entertain themselves with a number of riddles or " preguntas." [1]

After this Felicia prepares a magnificent spectacle for her guests. Richly-adorned barges containing nymphs in gorgeous attire and rowed by savages " crowned with roses," and tied to their rowing-benches with chains of silver, now appear, accompanied by most beautiful music,— the manœuvres concluding with a combat between the barges. This concluded, all return to the fountain, where they find the shepherd Tiranio, who sings some *rimas provenzales:*[2]

---

[1] On these riddles see the excellent article by Schevill, " Some Forms of the Riddle Question and the exercise of Wits in Popular Fiction and Formal Literature," 1911. (University of California Publications.)

[2] These *rimas provenzales* are certainly the most beautiful verses in the romance, and they have rarely been surpassed in Spanish poetry :

> Quando con mil colores devisado
> Viene el verano en el ameno suelo,
> El campo hermoso está, sereno el cielo,
> Rico el pastor, y prospero el ganado.
> Philomena por arboles floridos
> Da sus gemidos :
> Hay fuentes bellas,
> Y en torno dellas
> Cantos suaves
> De Nymphas y aves :
> Mas si Elvinia de alli sus ojos parte,
> Havrá contino hibierno en toda parte.
>
> Quando el helado cierzo de hermosura
> Despoja hierbas, arboles y flores,
> El canto dexan ya los ruyseñores,

Felicia now perceiving that night is approaching, " and it seeming to her that her guests had been sufficiently entertained for that day," made a sign, at which all were silent, and addressing the company, said that her guests could not complain of the treatment accorded them by her or by her nymphs; that all had been gratified except Narciso, " who was displeased with the treatment of Melisea,

> Y queda el yermo campo sin verdura;
> Mil horas son mas largas que los dias
> Las noches frias,
> Espessa niebla
> Con la tiniebla
> Escura y triste
> El ayre viste.
> Mas salga Elvinia el campo, y por do quiera
> Renovará la alegre primavera.
>
> *　　*　　*　　*　　*　　*　　*
>
> Si Delia en perseguir silvestres fieras,
> Con muy castos cuydados ocupada
> Va de su hermosa esquadra acompañada,
> Buscando sotos, campos y riberas;
> Napeas y Hamadryadas hermosas
> Con frescas rosas
> Le van delante,
> Está triumphante
> Con lo que tiene:
> Pero si viene
> Al bosque, donde caza Elvinia mia,
> Parecerá menor su lozania.
>
> Y quando aquellos miembros delicados
> Se lavan en la fuente esclarescida,
> Si allí Cynthia estuviera, de corrida
> Los ojos abajara avergonzados.
> Porque en la agua de aquella transparente
> Y clara fuente
> El marmol fino
> Y peregrino
> Con beldad rara
> Se figurara,
> Y al atrevido Acteon, si la viera,
> No en ciervo, pero en marmol convertiera.

and Tauriano with that of Elvina; these would, however, have to content themselves with hope." Here the book abruptly ends, while the history of other shepherds and shepherdesses, including the Portuguese Danteo and Duarda is again deferred to another part, which, " before many days, God willing, will be published."

It will be seen from the foregoing brief analysis that down to the fifth book the interest of the reader is well sustained; the various incidents follow each other quite logically,—they generally advance the action and the main thread of the story is well kept in view. In this respect the *Diana enamorada* is superior to the original of Montemayor, and a taste for pastoral fiction being once established, it is not strange that the work of Polo was successful, for of all books of its class its language is, perhaps, the least affected. Its prose style is graceful and flowing, and the poetry scattered through it is very beautiful, though, upon the whole, the work is inferior to the *Diana* of Montemayor.

It is greatly to be regretted that Polo, after so auspicious a beginning in the field of literature, forsook the Muse entirely, and never again turned to poetry. His case finds a parallel in the somewhat later poet Estéban Manuel de Villegas, who, after his brilliant debut in his *Eroticas* in 1617, like Polo, abandoned letters, and passed the remainder of his long life in the desperately dry and prosaic practice of the law. Both possessed the true poetic temperament, but, doubtless, lyric poetry held out no greater material inducements to its devotés in the sixteenth century than it does in the twentieth, and the lyric cry was stifled by the cry for bread. The *Diana enamorada* is one of the best of the pastoral romances; it also possesses the merit of not being too long; it is one of the few works in this species of literature that may still be read through with genuine pleasure.

THE "DIANA" OF TEXEDA.

In 1627[1] a third part of the *Diana* by Hieronymo de Texeda appeared in Paris.[2] It is a work of no merit what-

[1] Sixty-three years had elapsed between the publication of the *Diana enamorada* of Gil Polo and this continuation by Texeda, during which time most of the prose pastorals appeared in Spain. Texeda's work has only been considered in this place on account of its very close connection with the *Diana enamorada*. The Spanish translators of Ticknor, Tome III, p. 537, mention an edition of Texeda published at Paris in 1587. This is certainly a mistake.

[2] *La Diana de Montemayor nuevamente compuesto por Hieronymo de Texeda Castellano interprete de Lenguas, residente en la villa de Paris, do se da fin a las Historias de la Primera y Segunda Parte. Dirigida al excelentissimo Señor Don Francisco de Guisa Principe de Joinville. Tercera Parte, Paris, MDCXXVII.* Impresa a costa del Auctor. It is in two parts, bound in one volume, the first part containing three hundred and forty-six, the second part three hundred and ninety-four pages.

Of the life of Texeda we know nothing, but his address to the reader, in the above volume is interesting. It is as follows: "Discreto y curioso lector por hauer considerado la Historia de la Diana de Monte Mayor estar en la lengua Española imperfecta à causa de que en ella no se halla Terzera Parte impresa aunque los impresores Franzeses en su lengua la han echo à su fantasia tan apartada del intento e historias de la primera y segunda parte como se vee, me he resuelto à sacar la à luz puniendo con mi rudo estilo y corto entendimiento fin à las historias comenzadas, suplicando como suplico à los bien intencionados reziban la buena voluntad con la qual prometo en breues dias poner à luz todas las frases de hablar de la lengua Española para dar alguna clara noticia de los libros curiosos de ella à los aficionados à quien suplico me tengan por aficionadissimo criado." (signed) Texeda.

From the above reference to the French translations of the *Diana*, it seems that Texeda did not consider the *Diana enamorada* of Polo as a third part, although, as we shall see, he plundered it so shame-

ever, and is interesting only as being one of the boldest examples of literary theft in the history of any literature.

The story opens with Estela, Crimine and Parisiles
(characters introduced by Perez, in his continuation) going
to the village of Diana. They meet Amarantho, and tell
him of their going " á las obsequias de un pastor llamado
Delio." A story of Don Ramiro, brother of Alfonso of
Aragon, now follows, and on the next day at the fountain
of the Alders, they find Diana sitting, who, believing herself to be alone, sings:

> " El sufrimiento cansado
> De mi mal importuno y fiero
> A tal estremo ha llegado
> Que publicar mi cuidado
> Es el remedio que espero.
> Esclaua de un grave dolor
> Y dolorosa agonia
> Soy la que muere de amor,
> Oluidada de un Pastor
> Que de oluidado moria," etc.[1]

Hardly had Diana finished her song when a beautiful
shepherdess emerges from behind a myrtle and endeavors

lessly. As already observed, French translations of the *Diana* had
appeared in 1567, 1587 and 1592. I possess a copy of the latter translation, in which the *Diana enamorada* is much abridged, the poetry
being mostly translated into prose. The names of the authors of the
second and third parts are nowhere mentioned in the translations, so
that the reader is left under the impression that all these parts are
by Montemayor. The other work which Texeda announces is mentioned by Morel-Fatio (*Ambrosio de Salazar,* Paris, 1900, p. 143) and
again in the *Bull. Hispanique,* III (1901), p. 63. The title reads:
*Methode pour entendre facilement les Phrases et difficultez de la
langue Espagnole.* Par Hierosme de Techeda, Interprete Castillant.
Paris, 1629.

[1] If we compare with this the first poem in the *Diana enamorada*
of Polo (p. 3, ed. of Madrid, 1802) beginning: " Mi sufrimiento cansado," we find that Texeda began his plagiarism almost with the first
page of Polo, making only slight verbal changes.

to console her. It is Marfisa, " born of noble parents and placed in the position in which you see me by one of the various accidents of fickle fortune." Diana relates her griefs at the request of Marfisa, saying: " If you would hear what love can do, listen to a sonnet which my beloved Sirenus used to sing to me, in the time when his company was as pleasant to me as his memory now is bitter." She sings the sonnet, beginning:

"Que el poderoso Amor sin vista acierte," etc.[1]

Marfisa delivers a long discourse on the subject of love and jealousy, just as in the *Diana enamorada* of Polo, after which she recites a sonnet (p. 33), which is an exact copy from the latter work, except the fifth line:

"Nombrar llamas de Amor es desvario,"

which is omitted.[2]

Texeda next gives us Polo's sonnet (p. 15) beginning:

"Quien libre está, no viva descuydado."

The song printed by Texeda (p. 53), beginning:

Mientras el sol sus rayos tan ardientes

is the same as the *Rimas Provenzales* of Polo (pp. 17-21), the changes being very slight and always to the detriment of the verses.

It were useless to pursue this comparison in detail,—a

---

[1] Cf. with this the *Diana enamorada*, p. 10: " De cuyas (Amor) hazañas y maravillas en este mesmo lugar cantó un dia mi querido Syreno, en el tiempo que fue para mi tan dulce, como me es agora amarga su memoria." The sonnet which follows has been copied by Texeda verbatim,—only here and there changing a word. The name of the shepherdess Alcida is changed to Marfisa by Texeda.

[2] It is Polo's sonnet beginning: " No es ciego Amor, mas yo lo soy, que guio" (page 12).

few excerpts from the prose portion will show that this, also, is taken from Polo.

In the conversation of Marfisa with Delio (p. 58), the former says: " En gran cargo estoy á la fortuna, pues me ha no solo puesto en ocasion de ver la hermosura de Diana, mas en la presentia de aquel que juzgo merecedor de tal beldad, pero admiro me ver que tengas tan poca con la que mereze no solo por su beldad, mas por su raro entendimiento y discrecion ser estimada, pues la dexas hir solo un paso sin tu compañia, creo bien que siempre la tienes en tu coraçon." [1]

Again, on p. 66, Texeda has: " Pues me consta mi esposo Delio va 'en seguimiento de una hermosissima pastora que no ha mucho se apartó de nuestra compañia y por las muestras de aficion con que vi, la mirava en mi presençia, y suspiros que de lo profundo del corazon sacaua como aquella que sabe bien con quanta perseuerencia suele emprender lo que en el pensamiento se le pone, tengo por cierto, no dejara de seguir la pastora, aunque piense perder la vida, y lo que mas mi espiritu atormenta, es conozer la aspera y desamorada condiçion de la Pastora," etc.[2]

The sonnet in Texeda (p. 61) is the same as Polo's beginning

" No puede darme Amor mayor tormento,"

only the second word is changed. The Marcelio of Polo becomes Aristeo in Texeda, and recites the same story,— the shipwreck and subsequent rescue,—the name of Marfisa's younger sister, however, is Clarisea, instead of Clen-

[1] Cf. with this the passage in Polo (p. 12), beginning: " Delio, en gran cargo soy a la fortuna, pues no solo me hizo ver la belleza de Diana, mas conocer al que ella tuvo por meresceder de tanto bien," etc.

[2] These lines are copied from the *Diana enamorada*, p. 27.

arda, as in Polo. This whole episode is made ridiculous by Texeda, who causes the sailors, after they have bound Aristeo " hand and foot," to put a tallow gag in his mouth, after which they " put him upon the highest tree they could find." They then made off with Clarisea, leaving Marfisa behind, for some reason that is not explained. Marfisa calls, but Aristeo, his mouth full of tallow, is unable to answer, so she wanders inland and is lost. Aristeo kept the tallow in his mouth until rescued by some fishermen the next day, when he finds upon a poplar tree a sonnet, which the reader will find in the *Diana enamorada* (p. 49), with slight changes. The same characters now appear as in Polo's *Diana,*—Silvano and Selvagia, as well as Firmius and Faustus, " rivals for the hand of Diana."

I had carefully compared the two works and written down the passages in Texeda that were either similar or identical with those in the *Diana enamorada,* but it were a useless task to copy them here. Most of the poetry is taken from the latter work, as the verses: " Goze el amador contento " (p. 132), which are the *quintillas* in Polo (p. 178), and the *canciones* (p. 366): " Morir deviera sin verte," and " El Alma de alegria salte," which are in Polo (pp. 212-213). But Texeda has doubtless robbed others beside Polo. To give but a single instance: in Book x, p. 322, Texeda prints a sonnet beginning: " Tristezas, si el hazerme compañia," which is Lope de Vega's ninety-seventh sonnet in *La Hermosura de Angelica, con otras Rimas,* Madrid, 1602, fol. 284v.

It is only in the fifth book that Texeda begins to differ from Polo, and here the story of Amaranto and Dorotea is imitated from Perez. In the sixth book Parisiles relates the story of the Cid; in the seventh is told the story of the Abencerrages; in the ninth the story of Count Carlos and Lisarde, and the tribute of Mauregato.

The entire first four books of Texeda, as we have seen, are a plagiarism from the work of Polo, and these four books are all that are worth reading. Wherever a change has been made, either in the poetry or the prose of Polo, it has been for the worse. It seems almost incredible that at a time when the *Diana* of Polo was so well known and so widely read, anyone should have had the insolence to publish so flagrant a theft as an original work; and it is no less singular that so palpable a fraud should have escaped the critical acumen of a scholar like Ticknor. The second volume is dull and tedious in the extreme. The fourth part that is promised (p. 393), never appeared, doubtless because there was nothing left for Texeda to appropriate.[1]

[1] It appears that another *Tercera Parte de la Diana* was written by one Gabriel Hernandez, a resident of Granada, who, on January 28, 1582, obtained the privilege to print his work for ten years. This privilege was afterwards sold to Blas de Robles, bookseller, but the book, for some cause or other, was never printed. Menéndez y Pelayo, *Orígenes de la Novela,* I, p. cdxciii.

THE 'HABIDAS' OF HIERONIMO ARBOLANCHE.

AMONG the earliest of the imitations of the *Diana* was the *Habidas* of Arbolanche,[1] according to Gayangos. Unlike the *Diana,* however, it is written wholly in verse, which alone would make it rather doubtful whether its author took Montemayor's romance as his model. A brief analysis of the *Habidas* shows that it is rather a *novela caballeresca.* " It relates the story of Abido (hence the name of the romance), son of Gargoris, King of Spain. This son is exposed to wild animals and subsequently to the perils of the sea for the purpose of getting rid of him. He survives all dangers, however, and falls into the hands of a shepherd, by whom he is brought up. On the death of the King, Abido is returned to his mother and becomes King of Spain. While living among his flocks he falls in love with a shepherdess, which gives occasion to the author to introduce beautiful descriptions of nature. The work contains a number of eclogues and various shorter poems, *letrillas* and *villancicos,* which in sweetness and harmony are unsurpassed by the best verses of Montemayor." [2]

---

[1] *Los nueue Libros de las Hauidas de Hieronimo Arbolanche, Poeta Tudelano. Dirigidos a la Illustre Señora Doña Adriana de Egues y de Biamonte. En Çaragoça en casa de Iuan Millan.* 1566. 8°.

[2] Ticknor, *Historia de la Literatura española, traducida al castellano, con adiciones y notas críticas por D. Pascual de Gayangos y D. Enrique de Vedia,* Madrid, 1854, Vol. III, p. 538.

All that we know of Arbolanche [1] is that he was a native
of Tudela, in the province of Navarre.

The author, in his epistle to D. Melchor Enrico, 'su
Maestro en Artes' is very candid and modest concerning
his own poetical gifts, while his arraignment of some of
the Italian and Spanish poets is very amusing. He says
(I quote from Gibson's tr.) :

> O master mine, my will was never free
>   To find in printing books a great delight,
> But she who hath the power hath ordered me
>   To bring this ill-sung Book of mine to light;
> I grant I am not versed in poesy,
>   And only know that I know nothing right;
> And know as well that many know as little,
> So care not, if they praise me not, one tittle.
>
> I never chanted on Parnassus' height,
>   Nor ever drank the waters Cabaline:
> What Octave is or Sextain beats me quite,
>   Nor have I dealings with the Muses nine;
> Not mine the gift, like improvising wight,
>   At every step to vomit forth a line;
> I cannot verses on my fingers measure,
> Nor mouth two thousand fooleries at pleasure.
>
> I do not hire me sonnets to indite
>   For books that go to press in this our time:
> I do not ballads spin or tercets write,
>   Nor have one notion of impromptu rhyme:
> With echo-songs, in sooth, I'm puzzled quite,
>   To make them to the full note curtly chime:
> I do not medleys make, nor things at all
> That may be dubbed with name of Madrigal.

[1] On the reverse of the title-page is this inscription :
> "Ebro me produzió, y en flor me tiene,
> Mas my rayz de rio Calibe viene."

Which Gibson renders thus :
> Ebro produced me and keeps me fresh ever,
> But my stock hath its root on the Calibe river.

Journey to Parnassus, by Miguel de Cervantes, tr. by James Y.
Gibson, London, 1883, p. 380.

> I cannot use strange words or obsolete,
>   Nor am I read in books of chivalry:
> Nor can the names of blustering knights repeat,
>   Nor tell the tale of each stale victory;
> I know not what is meant by " broken feet,"
>   For mine own limbs are sound as sound can be;
> I cannot make some short and others long,
> Some very sweet and others very strong.

He is no admirer of the Italian measures introduced by Boscan:

> " Nor do I know to make my pen renowned
>   Upon my back bearing th' Italian theft."

His judgment of the great Catalan poet is very severe:

> " Nor can I verses make in Limousine,
>   Like Ausias Marc, which none can understand."

Montemayor is treated without pity:

> " Nor did I ever yet know to translate
>   So badly as the Lusian did erewhile,
> Nor know I *cancioneros* to create,
>   Mingling divine eke with the human style;
> Nor to *Diana,* first or second rate,
>   This heavy hand of mine could lay the file,
> Because all this to me seemed foolery,
> Nor make a ' Grove of various Poesy '."

He concludes:

> " I do not evil speak of men so high,
>   As if I thought I had sufficient grace
> To reach unto their lofty blasonry,
>   Still less to give myself a higher place;
> But since without much bitter raillery
>   None ever came off victors in the race;
> And since such famous men their weird must dree,
> What will the dolts and envious make of me?"

It is quite evident, as Mr. Gibson observes, that such a man was fair game for the shafts of Cervantes, and quite as evident that his rhinoceros hide was impervious to

any kind of contempt. Arbolanche is pilloried after this
fashion in " The Journey to Parnassus ":

> " On this came whizzing, like a bird on high,
>   A Book in prose and verse, shot by our foes,
> In bulk and height a very Breviary;
> From its extravagance in verse and prose,
>   'Twas Arbolanche's work, we well could guess,
>   His dull ' Avidas," heavy to the close."

Salvá says that he had always mistrusted the exaggerated
criticisms of Cervantes, and that this work (*The Havidas*)
confirmed his suspicions, for it follows from his very words
that Cervantes had never seen the book of Arbolanche,
which does not contain a line of prose, and is a thin volume
in small octavo, and not the ponderous tome Cervantes
makes it.[1] It is likely, as has been suggested, that Cervantes took the blank verse of Arbolanche as a kind of
disguised prose; at all events he seems to have had a score
to settle with the Navarrese bard and he did it. That the
verse of Arbolanche, however, deserves the favorable criticism of Gayangos, is shown by the following excerpts,
which fairly illustrate his style:

Cancion.

Partirme quiero, zagala
Partirme quiero de vos;
Mi zagala, á Dios, á Dios.

A Dios, montes, á Dios, prados,
A Dios, bosques y selva fria;
Que los lirios que aqui habia
En abrojos son tornados,
En ausencia mis cuidados
Partiendome yo de vos;
Mi zagala, á Dios, á Dios.

Dexo las cabrillas mias
Y el ganado en grande pena

---

[1] *Catálogo,* Vol. II, p. 18. Arbolanche also wrote a laudatory sonnet prefixed to the *Clara Diana a lo Divino* of Bartolome Ponce, published at Epila in 1580. *Ibid.,* No. 1944.

Al calor y á la berbena
Por essas silvas sombrias;
Voy á ver sus agonias,
Partiendome yo de vos;
Mi zagala, á Dios, á Dios.[1]

Cancion.

Soltaronse mis cabellos,
Madre mia,
¡Ay! ¿con qué me los prenderia?

Dicenme que prendo á tantos,
Madre mia, con mis cabellos,
Que ternia por bien prendellos,
Y no dar pena y quebrantos;
Pero por quitar de espantos,
Madre mia,
¿¡Ay! con qué me los prenderia?[2]

Cancion.

Ai Dios! qué cosa vana
Querer enamorarme
Pues ya no hai desviarme
De tí, linda Adriana.

Si de todas las nacidas
Me diesen á escoger,
Y las aun por nacer
Me fuesen ofrecidas,
Ai Dios! qué cosa vana
Seria enamorarme,
Pues ya no hai desviarme
De tí, linda Adriana.

Por tí en la noche oscura
Yo pierdo el dulce sueño,
Por tí con grande desdeño
Quejé yo de mi ventura;
Tu imagen soberana
Del todo pudo atarme,
Y asi no hai desviarme
De tí, linda Adriana.

---

[1] Ticknor, *Hist. of Spanish Lit.*, tr. by Gayangos, III, p. 538; Gallardo, *Ensayo*, I, col. 259.   L. 13 Gallardo reads: serena.

[2] Ticknor, *History*, tr. Gayangos, III, p. 538.

En prados y en oteros
Tu nombre he yo cantado,
De mí se han apiadado
Los animales fieros;
Mi anima malsana
Pudiste tu robarme,
Y ya no hai desviarme
De tí, linda Adriana.[1]

Cancion.

Caudaloso y fresco rio,
Tanto mal no merecí,
Siempre honré tus claras aguas
Y honraré mas desde aqui.
Ai, de tí! mas ai, de mí!

Siempre honré todas tus ninfas
Cuantas en tus prados ví,
Siempre de tus verdes ramos
Los mis cabellos ceñí,
Ai, de tí! mas ai, de mí!

¿Como, dime, consentiste
Que se fue y yo no me fué,
Aquel que con sus canciones
Tu ribera alegró así?
Ai, de tí! mas ai, de mí!

Aquel que con su zampoña
Las fieras atraía á sí,
Al son de la cual mil vezes
En sus haldas me adormí,
Ai, de tí! mas ai, de mí!

Abido, los tus ganados
Como pacerán sin tí?
Como cantaran las ninfas?
Dimelo, mi Abido, dí.
Ai, de mí! mas ai, de tí!

¿Porque, dime, en tu partida
Yo triste no me partí?
Y ¿porque si tu eres muerto
No me muero desde aquí?
Ai, de ti! mas ai, de mí![2]

[1] Salvá, *Catálogo*, II, p. 19.   [2] *Ibid.*, p. 19.

THE " TEN BOOKS OF THE FORTUNE OF LOVE."
BY ANTONIO DE LO FRASSO.

The next work in what may be called the cycle of the *Diana* was the *Ten Books of the Fortune of Love,*[1] by Antonio de lo Frasso, a Sardinian soldier, and was first published at Barcelona in 1573. This is the book that Cervantes characterizes as the most absurd book ever written, and though his genial and kindly nature was inclined to judge his contemporaries only too leniently, he is, for some unknown reason, especially severe upon Lo Frasso, although it appears that he fought with Cervantes against the Turks, and was present at Lepanto, on that memorable seventh of October, 1571 (Vol. II, p. 147).

" This book," said the barber, opening another, " is the *Ten Books of the Fortune of Love,* written by Antonio lo Frasso, a Sardinian poet." " By the orders I have received," said the curate, " since Apollo has been Apollo, and the Muses have been Muses, and poets have been poets, so droll and absurd a book as this has never been written, and in its way it is the best and the most singular of all of this species that have as yet appeared, and he who has not read it may be sure he has never read what is de-

---

[1] *Los diez Libros de la Fortuna d'Amor compuestos por Antonio de lo Frasso militar, Sardo, de la Ciudad de Lalguer, donde hallaran los honestos y apazibles amores del Pastor Frexano, y de la hermosa Pastora Fortuna, cō mucha variedad de inuenciones poeticas histori-adas. Y la sabrosa historia de don Floricio, y de la pastora Argen-tina. Y una inuencion de justas Reales, y tres triumphos de damas. Impresso en Barcelona, En casa de Pedro Malo Impressor.* [1573.] 8°. I have used the reprint in two volumes, London, 1740.

lightful. Give it here, gossip, for I make more account of having found it than if they had given me a cassock of Florence stuff.[1]

It is almost incredible that a Spaniard, and one of the editors of Lord Carteret's *Don Quixote,* should take the irony of the curate as a sincere expression of opinion. This praise, however, is one of the reasons assigned by Pedro de Pineda, the editor, for republishing it in England. But, if it were possible to be deceived by the words in *Don Quixote,* a perusal of the following lines in the *Journey to Parnassus,* should have dispelled all doubt as to the opinion of Cervantes:

"Look now if in the galley ye can see
  Some wretched bard, who may perchance by right
  A fitting victim for the monsters be!"
They found him in that man, *Lofraso* hight,
  Sardinian martial poet, who now lay
  Curled in a corner, and in dismal plight;
In his "Ten Books of Fortune" all the day
  Immersed; to add yet other ten to these
  He strove, to while the idle hours away;
Cried all the crew as one: "*Lofraso* seize!
  Down with him to the deep, and leave him there!"
  "Perdy," cried Mercury, "I do not please!
What! Can my soul the heavy burden bear
  Of casting to the sea such poesy,
  Although its foaming wrath demands our care?
Long live *Lofraso,* while the day we see
  Spring from Apollo's light, and men can smile
  And hold as wisdom sprightly fantasy!
To thee belong, *Lofraso* without guile,
  The epithets of subtle and sincere,
  My 'Boatswain' henceforth be thy name and style!"
Thus said Mercurius to our cavalier,
  Who in the gangway quick assumed his grade,
  Armed with a rattan, cutting and severe;

[1] *Don Quixote,* I, Chap. vi. Ormsby's tr.

Of his own verse, I fancy, it was made,
    And in a twinkling, how I do not know,
    Whether by Heaven's or *Lofraso's* aid,
On through the strait we safe and sound did go,
    Without immersing any poet there;
    Such strength lay in the good Sardinian's blow." [1]

Of Lo Frasso's life scarcely anything seems to be known beyond what he tells us on the title-page of this volume. [2] From another work, written two years earlier, in 1571, and in which the author informs us that he is writing it in the "middle of the raging Gulf of Leon," we learn that he had two sons, Alfonso and Cipion de lo Frasso, who were then, apparently, living in Barcelona. [3] Here, too, his pastoral romance was written. The work is composed principally of poetry, it being evidently a much easier task for the Sardinian bard to put his thoughts into generally bad verse, than into good prose. His shepherds and shepherdesses, moreover, must have been gifted with a vigor of constitution and a power of endurance far beyond that of the ordinary representative of that weary class. Their songs are often continued through ten or fifteen pages without any apparent sign of exhaustion; once, in the first book, Frexano, [4] the hero, beginning his song on page

---

[1] Gibson's translation, pp. 87-89.

[2] Nicolas Antonio, *Bibliotheca Nova,* II, p. 356, says: "Antonio Lofrasso, Sardus, Algueriensis, peota infimi subsellii, edidit: Diez Libros de Fortuna. Barcinone, 1573. Quod opus risu excipit D. Thomas Tamajus in 'Collectione librorum Hispanorum': atque item autorem inter eos, qui nullo subnixi Apolline, ac Musarum ingratiis operam versibus dedere, velut aliorum coriphaeum nominat, nasoque suspendit Michael de Cervantes Saavedra in metrico suo opere Viage del Parnaso nuncupato."

Frasso (Antonio de lo). *Comiença la Carta quel Autor enbia a sus Hijos y los mil y dozientos Consejos y Avisos discretos.* [Barcelona, 1571 ?] See Salvá, *Catálogo,* II, No. 2069.

[4] Under this name, as Clemencin surmised, is concealed the name

twenty, and singing until the thirty-seventh page,—the author says: " The shepherd growing weary of singing *octavas,* now changed his tune, and sang the following *tercetos."* The scene of the first five books is laid in Sardinia, near Lalguer, that of the remaining five in Barcelona.

The first book opens with a *carta* from Frexano " to his dear shepherdess Fortuna," followed by two sonnets and two *canciones,* then the letter is carried by Florineo, who sings a *cancion* while on his way. In the second book, Frexano makes a journey to Parnassus. The nine Muses appear, whom he addresses in verse, Minerva replying. This is followed by some curious verses, in which " hablan las potencias del cuerpo humano." First the tongue speaks, followed by the eyes, then the soul, the heart, the feelings, memory, thought, the will, affection, etc., finally ignorance, discretion, wisdom, married women, the widow, and last of all Amor. In the third book Frexano suffers the most frightful pangs of despised love, which ebb out in a *canto* that is continued for twelve pages. The fourth book contains a long poem in praise of Lalguer and its beautiful ladies, where Frexano meets his father and mother. The seventh book is not without interest, as it describes the festivities attending the marriage in Barcelona of Doña Mencía Faxardo y Çuñiga, daughter of D. Luys de Çuñiga y Requesens, under whom, apparently, Lo Frasso served at Lepanto on October 7. 1571 (Vol. II, p. 147). The seventh book also contains a long *Triumpho* in praise of fifty ladies of Barcelona, in imitation of the *Canto de Orfeo* of Montemayor and the *Canto de Turia* of Gil Polo. In the eighth book he relates the history of " Don Floricio and the beautiful shepherdess Augustina,"

of the author, Lofraso, which in the Sardinian dialect = el fresno, the Ash tree. Indeed, he tells us that Frexano was born in Lalguer (i. e. Alguer = Alghero in the northwestern part of Sardinia).

in which a *cancion* consisting of ninety-five stanzas is sung by Augustina. The whole work is absurd and perhaps nobody has read it through since Pedro Pineda corrected the proofs.[1]

A sonnet, " en lengua montañese Sardesca," may find a place here:

> Cando si dèt finire custu ardente
> Fogu qui su coro già mat bruxadu,
> Cun sanima misquina qui su fiadu,
> Mi mancàt vistù non poto niente.
>   Chiaru Sole & Luna relugente,
> Prite mi tènes tristu abandonadu,
> Pusti prode vivu atribuladu,
> Dami calqui remediu prestamente,
> Tue sola mi podes remediare
> Et dare mi sa vida in custa hora,
> Qui non morja privu de sa vitoria,
> In eternu ti depo abandonare,
> O belissima dea & senyora,
> De mè sa vida & morte pena y gloria.

(Vol. I, p. 284.)

The doughty bard, it seems, had no very exalted opinion of the weaker sex, to judge from the following song, which he puts into the mouth of Florineo:

> No pongas el pensamiento,
> Pasqual, jamas en muger,
> Qu-en pago de tu querer
> Te dará pena y tormento.

> Tiene tal naturaleza
> La que quiere ser servida,
> Si la quieres qual tu vida
> Te consume de tristeza.

[1] At the end of the second volume is this advertisement: "This individual Book is one of the greatest Rarities in the Spanish Tongue; being almost as hard to find as the Philosopher's Stone. Mr. Peter Pineda, the Spanish Master, has tried all Sorts of Methods to get it for Five and twenty Years. Cervantes gives it the highest Character in the World. Lib. I, Cap. 6."

En pocas verás firmeza,
Mudanse muy mas qu-el viento,
Qu-en pago de tu querer
Te daran pena y tormento.

Ni de veras, ni burlando,
No burles jamas con ellas,
Viudas, casadas, donzellas,
Dexalas por no yr penando:

Porque siempre variando,
Las veo hazer mudamiento,
Qu-en pago de tu querer,
Te daran pena y tormento, etc.   (Vol. I, p. 11.)

THE " FILIDA " OF MONTALVO.

A much better romance appeared in 1582 at Madrid in the "Shepherd of Fílida" of Luis Galvez de Montalvo.[1] Of the author's birth-place or life we know little more than what he tells us in this book. Speaking under the name of Siralvo, he says (p. 112, ed. of 1792) that he is not a native of the banks of the Tagus, but that his ancestors pastured their flocks by the Adaja, and that they removed thence to the Henares, upon the banks of which he was brought up, " i de alli, por favorable estrella, bevo las aguas del Tajo." [2]

Montalvo was attached to the house of Infantado, the lords of which had their principal residence in Guadalajara. In the ' Carta dedicatoria ' to his patron, Don Enrique de Mendoça y Aragon (the *Mendino* of the romance), he says: " Among the fortunates who know you and entertain

---

[1] According to Menéndez Pelayo there is a mutilated copy of this excessively rare first edition in the library of the Spanish Academy. The censura is dated Madrid, June 2, 1581. Other editions appeared at Lisbon, 1589; Madrid, 1590 and 1600; Barcelona, 1613, and Valencia, 1792. There are some laudatory verses by Luis Galvez de Montalvo prefixed to *La Vida, el Martyrio,* etc. . . . *de los gloriosos niños Martyres san Iusto y Pastor,* by Ambrosio de Morales, published at Alcalá, in 1568. Salvá, *Catálogo,* Vol. I, No. 299.

[2] The town on the banks of the Adaja, Menéndez y Pelayo conjectures to be Arévalo, and also surmises that a baptismal register of Luis, son of Marcos de Montalvo and his wife Francisca, born in 1549, refers to our author. The father of Siralvo, called Montano in the romance, was "mayoral del generoso rabadan Coriano," i. e. steward or something similar to the Marquis of Coria. *Orígenes de la Novela,* I. p. cdxcix.

friendly relations with you, I have been one, and indeed, one of the most fortunate; for desiring to serve you, my wish was fulfilled, and thus I left my house and other famous ones where I was requested to remain, and came to this, where I shall be pleased to die and where my greatest labor is to be idle, contented and honored as your servant."

In 1587 there appeared at Toledo [1] Montalvo's translation into Castilian of *Le Lagrime di San Pietro* by Luigi Tansillo, a Neapolitan gentleman who served D. Pedro de Toledo, Marqués de Villafranca, to whom Garcilasso dedicated his first eclogue. The latter mentions Tansillo among other Italian versifiers, in his twenty-fourth sonnet to Doña Isabel de Cardona.[2] According to Lope de Vega, in the prologue to his *Isidro,* Montalvo passed the latter years of his life in Italy. Speaking of Castillejo he says: " a quien (i. e. Castillejo) parecia mucho Luis Galuez Montaluo, con cuya muerte subita se perdieron muchas floridas coplas de este genero, particularmente la traducion de la Ierusalem de Torquato Tasso, que parece, que se auia ydo á Italia á escriuirlas para meterles las higas en los ojos." Again, in *La Viuda valenciana,* a comedia written before 1603, we read:

> *Leonarda.* Quien es este?
> *Oton.*   Es el Pastor
>   de Filida.
> *Leonarda.*   Ya lo se.

---

[1] In the *Primera Parte del Tesoro de divina Poesia.* . . . . Recopilado por Esteuan de Villalobos. En Toledo, en casa de Juan Rodriguez, Año 1587. *El Llanto de San Pedro* is now accessible in the *Floresta* of Böhl von Faber, Vol. III, No. 707, and in the *Romancero y Cancionero Sagrados* of D. Justo de Sancha, in the *Bib. de Aut. Esp.,* No. 668.

[2] See *Don Quixote,* ed. Clemencin, Vol. III, p. 14.

Oton.   Y Galuez Montaluo fue
con graue ingenio su autor.
Con Abito de San Juan
murio en la mar. . . .[1]

In his *Laurel de Apolo* he tells us that Montalvo met his
death " en la puente de Sicilia." [2] This expression, Clemencin says, must allude to some event well known at the
time, and agrees fully with the incident related by Fr.
Diego de Haedo in the " Dedication " of his *Topografia de
Argel:* " Era (dice por los años de 1591) Virei de Sicilia
el Sr. D. Diego Enriquez de Guzman, Conde de Alba de
Liste, el cual habiendo salido de Palermo á visitar aquel
reino, á la vuelta, como venia en galeras, hizò la cuidad
una puente desde tierra que se alargaba á la mar mas de
cien pies, para que alli abordase la popa de la galera donde
venia el Señor Virei, y desembarcase: y como Palermo es
la corte del reino, acudió lo mas granado á este recibimiento
. . . y con la mucha gente que cargó, antes que abordase
la galera dió el puente á la banda, de manera que cayeron
en el mar mas de quinientas personas . . . donde se ane-
garon mas de treinta hombres." As Clemencin adds:
" Una de ellas debió de ser el Pastor de Filida." [3]

As Menéndez Pelayo has justly remarked, " the Shep-

---

[1] *Comedias,* Parte XIV, Madrid, 1621, fol. 107, col. 1.

[2] Y que viva en el Templo de la Fama
Aunque muerto en la puente de Sicilia,
Aquel Pastor de Filida famoso
Galuez Montaluo, que la embidia aclama
Por uno de la Delfica familia
Dignisimo del arbol vitorioso:
Mayormente cantando
En lagrimas deshechos,
Ojos á gloria de mis ojos hechos.
                      Laurel de Apolo, ed. 1630, fol. 35v.

[3] *Don Quixote,* ed. Clemencin, Madrid, 1833, Vol. I, p. 147, note.

herd of Fílida is one of the best-written of the pastoral romances, though the least bucolic of them all." In the examination of Don Quixote's library, the curate had observed: " The one that comes next is ' The Shepherd of Fílida.' That is not a shepherd, said the curate, but a highly-polished courtier; let it be preserved as a precious jewel." [1] Montalvo and Cervantes were friends of long standing, and mention each other with praise in their works, [2] and from the fact that both were brought up on the banks of the Henares, it has been conjectured that they had known each other from youth, and that they were of about the same age. Of this, however, we have no proof.

It is probable that the *Filida* was written a number of years before it appeared in print. We have seen that Montalvo was known as a poet as early as 1568, and it is possible that his pastoral romance was written not long after that date. In the *Filida,* as in most works of this character, well-known persons appear in the disguise of shepherds, thus sacrificing the pastoral tone, for there is certainly very little that is bucolic about the ordinary occupations of Montalvo and his friends, as they are here depicted. The poet appears under the name Siralvo, Mendino is

[1] *Don Quixote,* Part I, Chap. vi. To the friendship subsisting between Montalvo and Cervantes is doubtless due, in part, this very favorable criticism of the *Filida*. Cervantes has introduced Montalvo in his *Galatea* under the name of Siralvo.

[2] Cervantes, in his *Galatea,* in the " Canto de Caliope," says :

> Quien pudiera loaros, mis pastores,
> Un pastor vuestro, amado y conocido,
> Pastor mejor de quantos son mejores,
> Que *de Filida* tiene el apellido !
> La habilidad, la ciencia, los primores,
> El raro ingenio, y el valor subido
> De *Luis de Montalvo* le aseguran
> Gloria y honor mientras los cielos duran.   (Book VI.)

Don Enrique de Mendoza y Aragon, his Mæcenas; Tirsi, *el culto Tirsi,* is Francisco de Figueroa; Pradelio is conjectured to be Don Luis Ramon Folch de Cardona, Conde de Prades;[1] the Arciolo of Book I, " que con tan heroica vena canta del *Arauco* los famosos hechos " (p. 154), is Alonso de Ercilla, and the Campiano is Dr. Campuzano, while Silvano is Gregorio Silvestre. The shepherdess Belisa, daughter of the very learned Lusitanian Coello (p. 59), who was a portrait painter (p. 122), is Doña Isabel Sanchez Coello, daughter of Alonso Sanchez Coello (*Origenes,* I, p. dvii). Under a slight pastoral disguise Montalvo (Siralvo) relates the story of his love for Fílida, and that of his Maecenas for Elisa. The scene is laid on the banks of the Tagus, perhaps in Toledo, as Menéndez Pelayo surmises. The incidents of the story are briefly as follows:

Mendino, a shepherd living on the banks of the Tagus, is enamoured of Elisa, " de antigua y clara generacion " and of beauty beyond compare. Mendino is, however, secretly loved by Filis, a beautiful nymph of the Tagus. One day, as Elisa, Filis, Cloris, Mendino and Galafron were sitting by a fountain amusing themselves with song, they are joined by the shepherds Bruno and Turino. And now Padelio, the noble and prosperous *rabadan* having died, there came to inherit his flocks his brother Padileo, " a gallant and discreet youth," who of course falls in love with Elisa, " greatly to the annoyance of Mendino and no less to Elisa." Elisa now writes a long letter to Mendino,

---

[1] See the learned introduction of D. Juan Antonio Mayans y Siscar to *El Pastor de Filida* compuesto por Luis Galvez de Montalvo, Gentil-Hombre Cortesano. Valencia, 1792. He gives a long list of works written in the manner of the *Diana* of Montemayor, many of which, however, are not pastoral romances. Mayans also mentions a pastoral by Francisco Rodrigues Lobo, in three parts, *A Primavera, O Pastor peregrino* and *O Desengañado.* They are written in Portuguese, and compare favorably with the best of the Spanish romances.

appointing a meeting-place. Here, one night, the latter is seen by the jealous Padileo, who, without more ado, asks the " beautiful and discreet Albanisa, widow of Mendineo " to become his wife. The thread of the story now grows somewhat involved,—Mendino, Corydon and Filardo visit the cave of the magician Sincero, who foretells Elisa's death; the latter dies as predicted and Mendino sings a dirge to her. The book closes with the couplet:

> " El mal que el tiempo hace,
> El tiempo le suele curar."

Alfeo, a shepherd lying upon the ground singing, is over-heard by Finea. Alfeo asks her whether she be not " a stranger and in love," to which she replies: " You might see this without asking me, by my dress, for one thing, *i en mi piedad, por otra.*" Alfeo is now informed that there is to be a general gathering of shepherds, " to honor the ashes of Elisa." They meet other shepherds and jour-ney to the spot, where they find Sasio, Filardo, Arsiano and the shepherdess Belisa, " hija del doctissimo Lusitano Coelio, los quatros mas aventajados en musica, i canto, que en las Españolas riberas se hallavan " (p. 59). Belisa and Sasio sing a *cantar*. In the plain stood a lofty pyramid of rich marble " covered almost wholly by ivy and branches." Alfesibeo sings an elegy, " interrupted at times by the most tender sighs." As Pradelio now arrives (llegió cansado), a young, robust shepherd, " de mas bondad que hacienda," Finea beams upon him, whereupon the jealous Filardo, " with features distorted by the power of love, and his brow covered with perspiration," arose and left, " but Pradelio paid no heed to this." Alfeo now sings a touching song, which moves all the listeners; Sileno, how-ever, " the venerable father of the deceased Elisa," com-mands the music cease, and proposes a wrestling match between the shepherds, followed by running, leaping and " tirar la barra," after which Galafron, " the tender and true lover of the deceased Elisa," sings some sad verses and the shepherds separate.

At the opening of the third book (or *Parte,* as it is called) Finea and Alfeo visit Siralvo. Directly they hear a flute and Siralvo sings the following rimas:

> Ojos a gloria de mis ojos hechos,
> Beldad inmensa en ojos abreviada,
> Royos que elais los mas ardientes pechos,
> Yelos que derretis la nieve elada:
> Mares mansos de amor, bravos estrechos;
> Amigos, enemigos en celada,
> Bolvéos a mi, pues solo con mirarme
> Podeis verme, i oirme, i ayudarme.
>
> Si me mirais, vereis en mi, primero,
> Quanto con Vos amor hace, i deshace;
> Si me escuchais, y oireis decir que muero,
> Y que es la vida que me satisface;
> Si me ayudais, lo que pretendo, i quiero,
> Que es alabaros, facil se me hace:
> En tan altas empressas alumbradme,
> Mis Ojos, vedme, oidme, i ayudadme. . . .   (p. 99.)

Filardo, the rival of Pradelio, now appears and up-braids Finea, saying: " ungrateful one, what seest thou in Pradelio more than in me? " Strangely enough, Finea asks him to sing, to which Filardo says: " And canst thou ask me to sing, seeing that I am dying? " " Then do as the swan does " (*pues haz como el cisne*) said Finea. Taking up his lyre, Filardo, " with three thousand sighs," begins to sing (*sacando la lira, con tres mil sospiros Filardo co-menzó a decir*). Siralvo, who is enamored of Filida, goes to the gardens of Vandalio, where Filida resides. Here he meets her friend Florela, and reads to her a poetical por-trait (*retrato en versos*) and the following sonnet:

> "Divino rostro, en quien está sellado
> El postrer punto del primor del suelo,
> Pues de aquel, en quien tanto puso el cielo,
> Tanto el pincel humano ha trasladado.
>
> Rostro divino, fuiste retratado
> Del que natura fabricó de yelo,
> O del que amor passando el mortal velo,
> Con vivo fuego, en mi dejó estampado.
>
> Divino rostro, el alma que encendiste,
> I los ojos que elaste en tu figura,
> Por ti responden, i por ellos creo.
>
> Rostro divino, que de entrambos fuiste
> Sacado, en condicion, i en hermosura,
> Pues tiemblo, i ardo, el punto que te veo." (P. 127.)

Siralvo now proceeds to Alfeo's cabin, who complains of the ungrateful Andrea, and thus, "while listening to the birds and to the gentle stream, with their cheeks resting on their hands, they fall asleep." Afterwards the shepherds visit the temple of Pan, where they meet Filida, and do not forget to eat and drink. Upon a large tablet they find "las leyes pastorales," and also "the art of making cheese. butter and other matters of more or less importance" (p. 162). Filida now sings a song, so beautiful "that the birds were hushed, the wind ceased, the fountain stopped, and I think the sun forgot its course, while the peerless Filida sang these verses" (p. 176). And now "todos son enamorados, pero no se puede decir de quien, que quando se sepa, sera un notable hechizo de Amor." Fanio, Delio and Liria sing a long Eclogue in the garden of the Temple. Meanwhile Siralvo is in a pitiable plight, "most of the time alone in his hut, amid cruel memories, hoping for death . . . stretched out upon the rocks he lay calling in vain for the beautiful Filida," and in the midst of these lamentations one day, "seated upon the dry trunk of a holly, he suddenly took out his rebeck, which was so forgotten, and with tender eyes accompanied his tears" to a song which he now sings (p. 219). Suddenly he sees a wounded stag,

pursued by two "gallardas cazadoras." One of them is
Florela. Siralvo dispatches the stag, then complains to
Florela of Fílida, and the former promises to intercede
for him. Andrea now appears and finally the shepherds all
proceed to the Temple of Diana, where the seven wonders
of the world are described. Siralvo again finds favor in
the eyes of Fílida, which makes him so happy that he cannot contain himself (en si mismo no cabia) and he recites
seven pages of verses, "quien gustare de oirlos, podrá
llegarse al Pastor, entanto que las Ninfas duermen; i quien
no, passe por ellos, i hallarálas despiertas" (p. 270). The
next song of Siralvo's, which I copy here as an illustration
of Montalvo at his best, is written in the old Castilian *redondillas,* which are handled with admirable grace:

> Filida, tus ojos bellos
> El que se atreve a mirallos,
> Mui mas facil que alaballos,
> Le será morir por ellos.
> Ante ellos calla el primor,
> Rindese la fortaleza,
> Porque mata su belleza,
> Y ciega su resplandor.
>
> Son ojos verdes rasgados
> En el rebolver suaves,
> Apacibles sobre graves,
> Mañosos y descuidados.
> Con ira, o con mansedumbre,
> De suerte alegran el suelo,
> Que fijados en el cielo,
> No diera el sol tanta lumbre.
>
> Amor que suele ocupar
> Todo quanto el mundo encierra,
> Señoreando la tierra,
> Tiranizando la mar,
> Para llevar mas despojos,
> Sin tener contradicion,
> Hizo su casa, y prision
> En essos hermosos ojos.

Alli canta, y dice: Yo
Ciego fui, que no lo niego;
Pero venturoso ciego,
Que tales ojos halló,
Que aunque es vuestra la vitoria,
En darosla fui tan diestro,
Que siendo cautivo vuestro,
Sois mis ojos, y mi gloria.

El tiempo que me juzgavan
Por ciego, quiselo ser,
Porque nó era razon ver
Si estos ojos me faltavan,
Será ahora con hallaros
Esta ley establecida,
Que lo pague con la vida
Quien se atreviere a miraros. . . .   (P. 285.)

The story now grows very tedious; there is a long discussion upon the merits of the two schools of Spanish
poetry,—the adherents to the old Castilian measures and
the Italianists,—and, in imitation of Montemayor, the
praises of celebrated Spanish women are sung. In the
seventh book Sasio, the musician, dies and has the honor
of having an epitaph written by " the famous Tirsi (Francisco de Figueroa) with his own hand," upon the trunk of
an elm tree. Orsindo, the former lover of Finea, now appears, and " all return to their first loves," *Alfeo i la encu-
bierta Andrea, a la suya, i Arsineo, vencido de la razon,
bolvió sus pensamientos a Silveria.* The work concludes
with a festival gotten up by Sileno, in which, among other
sports, the shepherds run at the ring, " a sport quite new
among shepherds."

It will be seen from this analysis of what incongruous
elements the book is composed; stories from Greek my-
thology are introduced, together with events from Spanish
history, and every occasion is taken to praise the house of
Mendoza. How far the vicissitudes of the shepherd Siralvo (his relations with Fílida are left unsettled at the close

of the romance) may agree with actual events in the life of Montalvo, we have no means of determining, as we know practically nothing of his personal history. But Montalvo loses no opportunity to extol the virtues and beauty of Fílida, and it is not improbable that her prototype played an important part in the life of the poet. We do not know the name of the lady, but from a poem by Montalvo's friend Lopez Maldonado,[1] we learn that the lady was for long years obdurate to the poet's attentions. From

> Pastor dichoso cuyo llanto tierno
>   a tanto que se vierte en dura tierra,
>   sin medida, sin tassa, y sin govierno.
>   *   *   *   *   *   *   *
>
> Ya te dio del descanso alegre llaue
>   Filida que entregada está y piadosa,
>   que es quanto bien Amor dar puede ó sabe. . . .
>   *   *   *   *   *   *   *
>
> Que la dulce consorte que te espera
>   y el talamo dichoso que te atiende. . . . .
>   *   *   *   *   *   *   *
>
> Mas ó Pastor amigo ó charo hermano
>   *   *   *   *   *   *   *
>
> Yo comence a cantar el dulce dia
>   de tu descanso. . . . .
>   *   *   *   *   *   *   *
>
> Dichoso tu que en puerto alegre y bueno
>   no temeras del mar fortuna fiera,
>   ni rayo ayrado de espantoso trueno.
> Ni mudança de bien, breue y ligera,
>   siguro gozaras lo ya adquirido
>   por medio y premio de una fe sinzera . . . . (fol. 186v).

these verses it follows, however, that Montalvo finally reached the goal of his longings.[2] When the marriage took

---

[1] "Epistola a un Amigo con quien se queria casar una Dama a quien auia seruido muchos años," in *Cancionero de Lopez Maldonado,* Madrid, 1586, fol. 185. It begins:

[2] I have not taken into account the "Epistola a un Amigo" (*Cancionero de Lopez Maldonado,* fol. 128 ff), as I am not at all certain that it was addressed to Montalvo.

place we do not know. All the verse in Maldonado's *Cancionero* was written before 1584, but the verses in question may have been, and most probably were, written long before that date, as it is equally probable that the *Fílida* was written long before its appearance in print in 1582.

Four editions of the *Fílida* had followed the first, in the next thirty years, down to 1613, when it was not printed again till 1792. And yet it is not easy to account for this popularity. It is true that Montalvo's short verses, the *glosas* and *redondillas,* are exceedingly graceful, and so eminent an authority as Menéndez y Pelayo declares that the *Fílida* is better than the reputation it enjoys, yet it is, on the whole, wearisome reading, and doubtless Cervantes's high praise of the work was influenced by his friendship for Montalvo, which here got the better of his judgment.

THE " GALATEA " OF CERVANTES.

THREE years afterwards, in 1585, Cervantes published his *Galatea*,[1] a pastoral romance in six books, and like so many of these works, this also was left unfinished, a fact which we need not regret, to judge by this very long fragment. It was the first work Cervantes published, though Montalvo had mentioned him as a poet three years before. It is, however, one of the poorest of all Cervantes's works, and gives little promise of his becoming the greatest name in the literature of Spain. He was now nearly thirty-eight years old, and, one might fairly say, had passed his *edad juvenil*, which could no longer be an excuse for the extravagances of his work. Many of the descriptions in the *Galatea* are certainly natural and graceful, and there are situations which are very skilfully managed; the whole showing a care in composition which he rarely bestowed on his later works; yet its general style is diffuse and rambling;

[1] *Primera Parte de la Galatea, dividida en seys libros. Cõpuesta por Miguel de Ceruantes.* Dirigida al Yllustrissimo señor Ascanio Colona, Abad de sancta Sofia (shield with the Colonna arms). Con privilegio. Impressa en Alcala por Iuan Gracian. Año de 1585. 8°, viii + 375 fols. Salvá, *Catálogo,* No. 1740. It has been alleged that the book first appeared in 1584; this is denied by Salvá, whose arguments will be found in his *Catálogo,* II, pp. 124-125. The matter is now set at rest by Mr. Fitzmaurice-Kelly, who discusses it with his usual competence and thoroughness, and shows conclusively that the edition of 1584 never existed. See his introduction to the *Galatea* of Cervantes, translated by H. Oelsner and A. B. Welford. Glasgow, Gowans & Gray, 1903. The second edition of the *Galatea* appeared at Lisbon in 1590. For other editions the reader is referred to the work just mentioned, pp. xlvi, *et passim.*

many of the pictures are greatly over-drawn, and there is a continual tendency to exaggeration. His erudite shepherds and shepherdesses delight in philosophical discussions, using the most polite and high-sounding phrases, often with an effect that is truly ridiculous. There seems to be no attempt at plot or connected narrative, and it is with the greatest difficulty that the reader keeps track of the various characters; a great number of shepherds and shepherdesses (some one has said there are no less than seventy-one) are brought successively upon the scene, and the maze of incidents is almost inextricable. " In mind and body these shepherds and shepherdesses are exceptionally endowed. They can remain awake for days. They can recite, without slurring a comma, a hundred or two hundred lines of a poem heard once, years ago; and the casuistry of their amorous dialectics would do credit to Sánchez or Escobar." [1] As Professor Fitzmaurice-Kelly truly says: " The pastoral *genre* was unsuited to the exercise of Cervantes's individual genius. . . . He longed to be an Arcadian, though he had no true vocation for the business."

Nor does Cervantes in these *primicias de su ingenio* reveal the slightest originality; he followed custom and borrowed freely from his predecessors in this field. " No careful reader of the Galatea can doubt that its author either had Sannazaro's *Arcadia* on his table, or that he knew it almost by heart. . . . His appreciation for the *Arcadia* was unbounded. . . . In the *Galatea* enthusiasm takes the form of conscious imitation." [2] It has been observed that

---

[1] Fitzmaurice-Kelly, *op. cit.*, p. xxxiii.

[2] *Ibid.*, p. xxix. Cervantes's residence in Italy had made him well acquainted with the language and literature of that country. His obligations to the *Arcadia* of Sannazaro had been pointed out long ago by Scherillo, in his excellent work *Arcadia di Jacobo Sannazaro*

Lisandro's song in the first book of the *Galatea* is imitated from the song of Ergasto on the tomb of Androgeo in the Arcadia. Lisandro's song begins:

> O alma venturosa
> Que del humana velo
> Libre al alta region viva volaste,
> Dexando en tenebrosa
> Carcel de desconsuelo
> Mi vida, aunque contigo la llevaste!
> Sin ti, escura dexaste
> La luz clara del dia,
> Por tierra derribada
> La esperanza fundada
> En el mas firme asiento de alegria:
> En fin con tu partida
> Quedó vivo el dolor, muerta la vida.

Compare with this Androgeo's song:

> Alma beata e bella
> Che da legami sciolta
> Nuda salisti ne' superni chiostri;
> Que con la tua stella
> Ti godi insieme accolta,
> E lieta uai schernendo i pensier nostri:
> Quasi un bel sol ti mostri
> Tra li piu chiari spirti;
> E coi uestigii santi
> Calchi le stelle erranti;
> E tra pure fontane e sacri Mirti
> Pasci celesti greggi,
> E i tuoi cari pastori indi correggi.
> (Fol. 21v, ed. Vinegia, 1556.)

A number of the prose passages in the *Galatea* are also pointed out by Scherillo, which bear such a close resem-

---

secondo i Manoscritti e le prime Stampe, Torino, 1888. Cervantes's imitations of the *Arcadia* are so many that Scherillo says: " Per dimostrare quanto numerose esse [derivazioni della *Galatea* dall' *Arcadia*] siano, ci vorrebbe addirittura una ristampa della *Galatea* coi richiami in margine dei passi dell' *Arcadia* " (p. ccliii).

blance to some in the *Arcadia* that there can be no doubt
that Cervantes drew freely on the latter work. The sixth
book of the *Galatea,* moreover, as this scholar has remarked
" è tutto imitato dalle ultime pagine dell' *Arcadia.*" [1] There
is much poetry scattered through the *Galatea,* and some of
it is very good, but there is much that is quite unworthy of
Cervantes. His sonnets will not bear comparison with
those of Montemayor; they are generally lacking in grace
and finish, and are not redeemed by any strikingly beautiful
thoughts. And it is certainly strange that one who loved
the old Spanish ballads so well and who knew most of
them by heart, should have failed to give us a single composition in this measure.

Cervantes always cherished a singular affection for the
Galatea, with which he made his debut in the world of
letters. Yet no one, surely, was better aware of its excessive
sentimentality and unnaturalness than he himself. Nearly
thirty years later, in his " Colloquy of the Dogs," he speaks
as follows of these pastorals: " In the silence and solitude
of my siestas, it occurred to me among other things that

---

[1] Scherillo, *Arcadia di Sannazaro,* pp. ccli, and foll. The beginning
of the *Carta* of Timbrio to Nisida in Book iii, bears a striking re-
semblance to the letter to Cardenia in Book ii of the *Diana* of Perez:

> *Galatea:* " Salud te envia aquel que no la tiene,
> Nisida, ni la espera en tiempo alguno,
> Si por tus manos mismas no le viene."

Cf. the letter in the *Diana:* " Salud te embia el que para si, ni la
tiene, ni la quiere, si ya de ti sola no le viniesse," etc. One of the
Epistolas of Diego Hurtado de Mendoza begins:

> " A Marfira Damon salud envia,
> Si la puede enviar quien no la tiene,
> Ni la espera tener por otra via." Ed. Knapp, p. 101.

It is probable that this is the source of Perez, and perhaps also of
Cervantes, who, in the *Galatea* (Bk. vi) represents a number of shepherds visiting the tomb of *Meliso* (Mendoza) and reciting in verse
a lament to his memory.

there could be no truth in what I had heard tell of the life
of shepherds,—of those at least about whom my master's
lady used to read when I went to her house, in certain
books all treating of shepherds and shepherdesses; and telling how they passed their whole life in singing and playing
on pipes, reeds, rebecks, and other strange instruments. I
heard her read how the shepherd Anfriso[1] sang divinely
in praise of the peerless Belisarda, and that there was not
a tree on all the mountains of Arcadia upon whose trunk
he had not sat and sung from the moment Sol quitted the
arms of Aurora, till he threw himself into those of Thetis,
and that even after black night had spread its sable wings
over the face of the earth, he did not cease his well-sung
and better-wept complaints. Nor did I forget the shepherd
Elicio,[2] more enamored than bold, of whom it was said that
without attending to his own love or his flock, he entered
into the griefs of others; nor the great shepherd of Filida,[3]
unique painter of a portrait, and who had been more faithful than happy; nor the anguish of Sireno and the remorse
of Diana, and how she thanked God and the wise Felicia,
who, with her enchanted water, undid the maze of en-
tanglement and difficulties.[4] I used to remember many
other books of this same kind, but they were not worthy
of being remembered. . . . All these things enabled me to
see the more clearly the difference between the habits and
occupations of my masters and the rest of the shepherds
in that quarter, and those shepherds of whom I had heard
read in the books. For if mine sang, it was not tuneful and
finely-composed strains, but a " Ware the Wolf," and

[1] A reference to the *Arcadia* of Lope de Vega, in which Anfriso is
in love with Belisarda.

[2] Elicio, one of the shepherds in the *Galatea,* is Cervantes himself.

[3] Refers to the *Pastor de Filida* of Cervantes's friend Montalvo.

[4] An allusion to the *Diana* of Montemayor.

" Where goes Jenny," and other similar ditties, and not to the accompaniment of hautboys, rebecks or pipes, but to the knocking of one crook against another, or of bits of tile jingled between the fingers and sung with voices not melodious and tender, but so coarse and out of tune, that whether singly or in chorus they seemed to be howling or grunting. They passed the greater part of the day in hunting up their fleas or mending their brogues; and not one of them was named Amarilis, Fílida, Galatea or Diana, nor were there any Lisardos, Lausos, Jacintos or Riselos,[1] but all were Antones, Domingos, Pablos or Llorentes. And from this I concluded what I think all must believe, that all those books [about pastoral life] are only fictions ingeniously written for the amusement of the idle, and that there is not a word of truth in them, for, were it otherwise, there would have remained among my shepherds some trace of that happy life of yore, with its pleasant meads, spacious groves, sacred mountains, beautiful gardens, clear streams and crystal fountains; the tender terms, as decorous as they were ardently spoken, with here the shepherds, there the shepherdesses all woe-begone, and the air made vocal everywhere with flutes and pipes and flageolets." [2]

In accordance with the custom of the time, Cervantes introduces a number of poets as shepherds, he himself appearing as Elicio;[3] it is also the general opinion that Galatea was a young lady of Esquivias, Doña Catalina de Palacios Salazar y Vozmediano, who soon afterward became his wife. The *Galatea* has generally been considered as an

---

[1] *Lisardo* was the pastoral name of the poet Luis de Vargas Manrique; *Lauso* that of Barahona de Soto, and *Riselo* that of Pedro Liñan de Riaza.

[2] See also *Don Quixote*, Part II, Chap. lxvii.

[3] Navarrete (*Vida de Cervantes*, Madrid, 1819, p. 66) says: " Under the names of Tirsi, Damon, Meliso, Siralvo, Lauso, Larsileo and Arti-

offering to this lady, and having accomplished the purpose
for which it was written, it was never concluded.[1] This
may or may not be true; the fact is that Cervantes was married to Da. Catalina de Palacios on December 12, 1584,
and the probability is that, being now married, he sought
some more remunerative occupation than the writing of
pastoral romances; at all events, within six months we find
him at Madrid, where he was then engaged in writing
comedias for the *corrales*. Herein we know that he was
not successful, and he soon turned his hand to anything
that promised him a living, beginning that long struggle
with poverty from which only death finally set him free.

With all the evident care which Cervantes bestowed on
the *Galatea,* it is a dull book; the only episode of interest
is the recital of Timbrio's adventures. The story in brief
is as follows:

" Timbrio, being challenged to a duel by another knight,
sets out for Naples. Silerio, his friend, being detained by
sickness, follows after some days, and being left on the
coast of Catalonia by the galley in which he sailed, he per-
ceives, on the next morning, a crowd following a man who
is being led to execution. It is Timbrio, who had been
captured during a descent made upon a robber band by
which he had been waylaid and held. Silerio rescues him,
and both finally escape to Naples, where the duel is to be
fought. Here Timbrio falls in love with Nisida; Silerio,

doro, Cervantes introduced into his story Francisco de Figueroa,
Pedro Lainez, D. Diego Hurtado de Mendoza, Luis Galuez di Montalvo, Luis Barahona de Soto, D. Alonso de Ercilla and Micer Andres
Rey de Artieda, all friends of his and very celebrated poets of that
time." Of these *Tirsi* is certainly Figueroa, Diego Hurtado de Mendoza also calls himself *Damon* in his verse; of Lainez I am unable to
say what his poetical name was; the last four pastoral names cor-
respond with the poetical names of the poets mentioned.

[1] Ticknor, *History of Spanish Literature,* Vol. II, p. 119.

disguised as a buffoon, is received into Nisida's house, where he pleads the cause of Timbrio, at the same time falling in love with Nisida, while Blanca, her sister, becomes enamoured of him. Nisida returns the affection of Timbrio. All now proceed to the duelling ground, Nisida's parents going also, accompanied by Blanca. Nisida, however, had remained behind some distance, and had arranged with Silverio to give her a signal from afar, so that she might know that Timbrio were safe. After the duel Silverio appears, but neglects to wear the sign. Nisida falls in a swoon; all believe her dead, and Timbrio departs for Spain, while Silerio returns to become a hermit, the two sisters wandering afterward to seek Timbrio. The vessel on which Timbrio sailed, however, is obliged by a violent storm to return to Gaeta, departing again a few days afterward. One day while Timbrio is singing on the vessel, Nisida suddenly appears beside him, accompanied by Blanca. She relates how, with an attendant, and in pilgrim's attire, she went to Gaeta, and embarked on the vessel after its return from the storm, intending to seek Timbrio at Xeres. Shortly afterward some Turkish galleys are seen in the distance, which greatly increase in numbers, and attack Timbrio's vessel. A desperate fight ensues, which lasts for sixteen hours, when Timbrio's vessel is finally captured by the corsairs, who are led by Arnaut Mami. They are all taken aboard a Turkish galley, subjected to the most cruel treatment, and are ready to give up all hope, when a terrible storm suddenly arises, which is so violent that it scatters the Turkish vessels, sinking many of them and driving the Arnaut's galley toward the Catalonian coast. As the storm increases in fury, the Turkish leader requests the Christians to invoke their saints and Saviour to shield them from destruction. Their prayers are not in vain, for the storm abates, but the next morning they find themselves so close to the coast of Catalonia that escape is impossible, and they decide to land, ' for love of life made slavery appear sweet to the Turks,' who are promptly murdered by the Catalonians. This takes place on the very spot where a short time previously Silverio had saved Timbrio's life."

This, it must be admitted, is a rather improbable story, though there are passages written with much spirit—passages in which there is just a faint foreshadowing of the great Cervantes of the *Don Quixote,* for here he was inspired by an episode in his own life—his capture by this same Arnaut Mami—an adventure which he was again to turn to good account afterward.

The *Galatea* was not successful, and little blame is to be attached to the public for not waxing warm over these erudite, fictitious shepherds.[1] And yet, at this time, as if endowed with the gift of prophecy, the poet Galvez Montalvo foretold the coming of the name that was to go down through all the ages.[2] Surely only a seer's eye could discover such promise in this somnolent pastoral romance.

[1] That the *Galatea* enjoyed some popularity in its day, however, is shown by the two *romances* which appeared at Valencia in 1591 (Gallardo, *Ensayo,* I, p. 1396), written by Juan de Salinas; they are published in the *Romancero general* (Duran, II, pp. 471, 472), and in the *Poesías del Dr. D. Juan de Salinas,* Seville, 1869, Vol. I, pp. 24, 28.

[2] In the following sonnet, prefixed to the first edition of the *Galatea:*

> Mientras del yugo sarracino anduvo
> Tu cuello preso y tu cerviz domada,
> Y alli tu alma al de la Fe amarrada
> A mas rigor mayor firmeza tuvo,
>   Gozóse el cielo; mas la tierra estuvo
> Casi viuda sin ti, y desamparada
> De nuestras musas la real morada,
> Tristeza, llanto, soledad mantuvo.
>   Pero despues que diste al patrio suelo
> Tu alma sana y tu garganta suelta,

Cervantes, indeed, seems always to have been proud of this first child of his genius, for he often recurs to it in later years; [1] no less than five times he promises a conclusion to the *Galatea,* and there may be concealed beneath its pastoral allusions a significance which the second part might have revealed and the *Galatea* "thus have won the full measure of grace that is now denied it." As late as 1615, one year before his death, he says in the preface to the second part of *Don Quixote:* " thou mayest expect the *Persiles,* which I am now finishing, and also the second part of *Galatea.* The *Persiles* he finished four days before his death, writing with the last strokes of his pen, the graceful and grateful dedication to the Count of Lemos. But like *El famoso Bernardo* and *Las Semanas del Jardin,* the second part of the *Galatea* was never written, or if any portion of it was written, it has disappeared utterly. Perhaps we need not regret its loss; indeed, there is infinite consolation in the knowledge that it could not possibly have added to the reputation of its author.

> De entre las fuerzas barbaras confusas,
>   Descubre claro tu valor el cielo,
> Gózase el mundo en tu felice vuelta
> Y cobra España las perdidas musas.

[1] It must have given Cervantes not a little satisfaction to see the *Galatea* praised by his great rival Lope de Vega. In one of his comedias, *La Viuda Valenciana,* written before 1604, we read:

> *Oton:* aqueste es la *Galatea,*
>   que si buen libro dessea
>   no tiene mas que pedir.
>   Fue su autor Miguel Ceruātes,
>   que alla en la Naual perdio
>   una mano.   Act I, fol. 107, ed. of 1621.

"THE ENLIGHTENMENT OF JEALOUSY," BY LOPEZ DE ENCISO.

In the following year (1586) a romance appeared entitled "The Enlightenment of Jealousy," by Bartholomé López de Enciso.[1] Of its author we know nothing more than he himself tells us on the title-page: that he was a native of Tendilla, a small town in the province of Guadalajara. We hear of him again in 1598,[2] and at the festival of Corpus Christi at Seville in 1618, the actor Juan de Morales Medrano and his wife Jusepa Vaca and their company of players represented the *auto* entitled *La Montañesa,* by Bartholomé de Enciso.[3] Whether this dramatist and Bartholome Lopez de Enciso are one and the same person, however, I have no means of determining.

---

[1] *Desengaño de Celos. Compuesto por Bartholome Lopez de Enciso, natural de Tendilla. Dirigido al illustrissimo Señor Don Luys Enrriquez, Conde de Melgar* [Device, figure of a man]. *Con Privilegio. Impresso en Madrid en casa de Francisco Sanchez.* Año, 1586, small 8°, 321 leaves. In a MS. note Ticknor says: "This is one of the rarest books in Spanish literature." I have also used a copy in the Göttingen University library. The title of the work is thus translated by Braunfels: "Der Titel bedeutet so wohl die Widerwärtigkeiten welche die Eifersucht mit sich bringt, als die Erkenntnis der Thorheiten die sie uns begehen läszt." *Don Quixote,* tr. by Braunfels, Vol. I, p. 89, note. This also, was one of the volumes in Don Quixote's library. *Don Quixote,* ed. Clemencin, I, p. 145.

[2] In that year he contributed a sonnet to Cristobal Perez de Herrera's *Discurso del Amparo de los legitimos pobres,* etc., Madrid, 1598. Pérez Pastor, *Bibliografía Madrileña,* I, p. 313.

[3] Sanchez-Arjona, *Anales del Teatro en Sevilla,* Sevilla, 1898, pp. 192, 194, 195. Barrera (*Catálogo,* p. 131) thinks that our author may be the Bartolome de Anciso, author of the comedia *El Casamiento*

In the " Epistola al Lector " our author says that, having observed the disastrous effects of jealousy, he has endeavored to ascertain " whether in any way this confessed evil might not be rooted out and banished from the breasts of those who have cherished it. And among the many things that my fancy proposed to me, I chose as best for my purpose, to write of the disastrous results that have been produced by jealousy . . . and, likewise, to show the infinite advantages that result from its absence."

The author feared, inasmuch as his work consisted " merely of admonitions and counsels," that, " in view of the debased taste of these times," his work would not receive the attention that was its due. He therefore clothed it in a pastoral style " to render it agreeable to all readers, never swerving, however, one iota from my main purpose, which is to expose the vanity and absurdity of jealousy.

con *Zelos y rey Don Pedro de Aragon,* published in *Parte treinta y tres de Comedias nuevas nunca impressas, escogidas de los mejores Ingenios de Espana.* Madrid, 1670. (Ibid., p. 699.) Barrera also puts the query whether this may be the writer referred to by Cervantes in the *Viagc del Parnaso,* as "gloria y ornamento del Tajo, y claro honor de Manzanares." Two of the laudatory poems prefixed to the *Desengaño de Celos* praise its author in the most extravagant fashion. The licenciado Huerta says:

> " Bien puede su memoria eternizarse
> Concediendole nombre de diuino,
> Pues con diuino espiritu se muestra.
> Y bien pueden sus obras celebrarse
> Mejor que la Thebayda de Papino
> Con honrra suya, de su patria y nuestra."

The licenciado Don Luys de Barrionueuo says:

> " Pues tiene de consejos tanta sobra
> Y con su estilo esta tan leuantada
> Que se puede llamar obra del cielo."

We are inclined to doubt whether even Enciso himself believed all this.

He continues: " Having written this first part, I had determined to use it only for my own contemplation and that it
should remain hidden . . . but communicating it to some
of my friends, they were of the opinion that I should publish it. And not only this, but so much did they persuade
me that I was obliged to yield to their pleasure and their
prayers." Besides, he says, it had been read by *cierta persona* " whom he could not fail to obey " and by whom he
was commanded to publish it. He calls it the work of a
young man and the first upon which he has labored, and
begs that it may be received as such and that its errors may
be pardoned. This, he concludes, would give him courage
to publish the second part. Surely this was frank enough
and modest enough, yet his readers seem to have considered his errors unpardonable, for he never had an opportunity to publish the second part.

In this romance the scene is again laid " upon the lovely
banks of the golden Tagus," along which " the pitiful shepherd Laureno " pursues his way, " having left on his right
hand his beloved village." Suddenly he hears voices as of
men quarreling and presently sees two shepherds with
drawn knives about to rush upon one another. At the same
moment a beautiful shepherdess appears from behind a
clump of trees, and pacifies the bellicose shepherds, saying:
" as you are both unbeloved (*desamado*) of the shepherdess
Clarina, there is no reason why you should be jealous of
each other." Then, " desiring to reconcile them, she took
them each by the hand and sat down with them close by a
sweet spring, which was there." This being seen by the
lorn Laurenio, " together with what he had seen and heard
of the shepherds, brought upon him the most terrible despair: Knowing jealousy only without ever having been
loved, it had driven him to such a point, that recalling the
happy time in which he enjoyed the most pleasant life that

one can imagine, and seeing himself not only deprived of that happiness, but exiled from his native land, and so filled with grief without any hope of remedy; with an anguish which seemed to rend his soul, uttering loud cries and heaving passionate sighs, he let himself fall upon the earth, deprived of all senses." Here he lay, " uttering such cries and making such sad echoes, that the two shepherds with the charming shepherdess, hearing his laments, had arisen to see what it was." They found him " writhing on the ground, with clenched fists, and gritting his teeth in such a manner that they became afraid." [1]   Recovering from their fear, " they endeavored to restore him to his senses, but seeing that these efforts were in vain, one of the shepherds returned to the fountain and bringing some water in a cup, dashed it into his face." Seeing that he is about to recover, they withdraw amongst the trees, where they can observe his actions. They see him take a letter from his scrip, " and with violent rage, he tears it to pieces; then drawing forth a rebeck [2] that was out of tune, and attuning it in harmony with his sighs, making a very direful and lamentable sound, he began with the sadness with which the hoarse swan is wont to sing in his last moments, to recite these verses." After finishing his song, he throws away his rebeck, " lest the memory of it should increase his grief, although it is already so great that it allows of no increase." Then " he draws forth from his scrip a yellow spoon of smooth box-wood, beautifully carved, and

[1] " Llegando donde estaua, quedaron admirados, el qual como quien de mal de coraçon esta tocado, por el suelo apriesa se rebolcana, haziendo sus bestiduras pedaços, apretando las manos, y vatiendo los dientes tan fuertemente, que grande espanto en los tres que le mirauan ponia, y llegandose a el, mouidos de compasion, procuraron boluerle en si."

[2] Rebeck, in Spanish, *rabel,* a small three-stringed lute of Moorish origin. See *Don Quixote,* ed. Clemencin, Vol. I, p. 237.

throwing it far from him," says: "thou spoon, with which that mouth, as beautiful as it is false, was wont to eat, no longer shalt thou be in my company," etc.

Surely absurdity has reached its very verge in such stuff as this. And so this history continues its weary course through six books. On fol. 96, Rosano, a shepherd, relates the story of "the unhappy fate of the Lusitanian prince." [1] In Book IV the shepherds discourse upon Polyphemus, Herakles and Dejanira, Medea, Dido, Hero and Leander, Piramus and Thisbe, Tereus, Progne and Philomela, Paris and Enone, etc., and otherwise display a knowledge of ancient lore, while in Book V, as in nearly every one of these romances that followed the *Diana,* the shepherds are conducted by a nymph to the Temple of Diana, where they see the statues of Charles V., Philip II., Don John of Austria and Philip III.

It is one of the dullest books imaginable, and the curate in *Don Quixote* (Part I, Chap. vi) showed it no mercy. It is written in a cumbrous and diffuse style, the monotony of which is only relieved, now and then, by some absurdity.

Of the verse scattered through the book, and which is decidedly better than the prose, a few specimens follow:

Laurenio's Song.

Del resplandor del Sol, y las estrellas,
De la veldad mayor que tiene el cielo
Un retrato purissimo en el suelo,
Mostrandonos esta mil gracias bellas,
Quien quiera ver cifrada del altura
La hermosura
En un humano
Y souerano
Rostro y talle,
No a buscalle

---

[1] Prince Ferdinand of Portugal, who died in captivity at Fez, in 1443, and upon whose tragic fate Calderon has founded one of his best comedias, *El Príncipe constante.*

Al cielo suba; vengase à este prado,
Do todo lo vera muy acauado.

   Quien pretendiese ver la perficion,
Y donde remató naturaleza
El estremo mas alto de la belleza,
Donayre, gracia, brio, y discrecion,
Y quien de graudedad, y de valor
Desea el primor
Ver con los ojos,
Dando en despojos
Por vista tal
La mas ynmortal,
No canse en otras partes; à este fuente
Venga, do lo vera mas excelente.

   Vera aqui en el ynbierno riguroso
Conuierte en agradable primauera,
Y quien subgeta y rinde toda fiera,
Con solo un mirar de ojo amoroso,
Vera quien del calor del seco Estio,
Un grato frio
Su vista ofrece,
Y reberdece
Las florecillas
Que ya amarillas
Estan del rojo Sol con ser tocadas,
De sus hermosas plantas delicadas (fol. 66).

Sonnet.

   Hermosa y dulce fuente, verde prado,
Floridos campos, arboles sombrios,
A donde solia yo los males mios
Cantar en vuestros troncos recostado.
   Si con lagrimas hize en lo passado
Crecer las aguas destos claros rios,
Escuchad de mi muerte los desuios,
Y el bien à que mi suerte me ha llegado.
   Oyreis de amor hazañas nunca oydas,
De fortuna grandissimas mudanças
Y de un pastor el hado venturoso.
   Pues quien puede quitar oy cien mil vidas,
Gusta de darme firmes esperanças
Que me ha de ver muy presto aqui gozoso (fol. 79).

" And now the doleful Fenisa, playing upon a delicate though husky bag-pipe, with more sadness than the widowed turtle-dove, with faint voice drawn from her sad bosom, sang the following verses " :

> Hermoso, ameno y agradable valle
> Eras en todo tiempo al alma mia,
> Quando mi dulce Flaminio en ti viuia,
> Dandote el ser que él solo podia dalle.
> Mas ya no ay gusto en ti, y querer buscalle
> Mayor locura y torpedad seria
> Que pedir vivo fuego al agua fria
> O que al bulgo querer hazer que calle.
> Para todos produces vellas flores,
> A todos tu sombria da contento,
> Y tu yerua sustento a los ganados.
> Renuebanse en mirarte los amores,
> Suspendes á los tristes el tormento.
> Y á mi sola me doblas los cuydados.
>
> O fiera muerte que mi bien llebaste,
> Insana, mira ya que conseguiste,
> Pues por tu causa todo queda triste,
> Despues que el cielo al suelo le quitaste.
> Si solo un cuerpo piensas que priuaste
> De vida con el golpe que hiziste,
> Engañaste, qui á dos la muerte diste,
> Ya todo el orbe sin el sol dexaste.
> Terrible nuncio de mi dura muerte,
> No pretendas jamas mi compañia,
> Que muero aunque es de viva mi diuisa.
> Al punto feneci que mal tan fuerte
> Supe pues de contino residia
> En la de Flamio el alma de Fenisa (fol. 243-244).

" No pudo pasar adelante con su canto, la triste pastora : mas llegando aquestos postreros versos : hecho un nudo en la garganta, faltando a los penados ojos humor, que distilar : solloçando, y aun paresciendo ahogarse con la pena : cayendosele la çampoña de las manos, desmayada, le fue forçado dexar se tender sobre la verde yerua."

THE NYMPHS AND SHEPHERDS OF THE HE-
NARES, BY BERNARDO GONZALEZ
DE BOUADILLA.

THE next pastoral romance to make its appearance was the *Nymphs and Shepherds of the Henares,* by Bernardo Gonçalez de Bouadilla, a student at Salamanca.[1] This also was one of the volumes in Don Quixote's famous library,[2] but the priest shows its short shrift and immediately hands it over to the secular arm of the housekeeper, to be committed to the flames; nor does it find greater favor at the hands of Cervantes in the *Viage del Parnaso,* where it accompanies another pastoral romance, *The Shepherd of Iberia,* by Bernardo de la Vega:

> For many hast thou raised to Fortune's height,
>   Who still in dark Oblivion's den should be,
>   Without or Sun or Moon to give them light;
> *Iberia's shepherd,* grand Bernardo he
>   Had in thy mission neither lot nor part,
>   Who bears La Vega's surname and degree;
> Thou hadst an envious, careless, sluggish heart,
>   And at *Henares' Nymphs and Shepherds* fine,
>   As if they were thy foes, didst hurl thy dart;
> And yet, within that great sheepfold of thine,
>   Worse poets hast thou, who must sweat and strain,
>   If they would better be, as I opine! [3]

[1] *Primera Parte de las Nimphas y Pastores de Henares. Diuidida en seys libros. Compuesta por Bernardo Gonçalez de Bouadilla Estudiante en la insigne Vniuersidad de Salamāca. Dirigida al Licenciado Guardiola del Consejo del Rey nuestro Señor.* Con Privilegio. Impressa in Alcala de Henares, por Juan Gracian. Año de MDLXXXVII. A costa de Iuan Garcia mercader de Libros. 8°, 215 ff.

[2] *Don Quixote,* Part I, Chaps. vi and ix. It is a volume of such extraordinary rarity that Clemencin, in his note to the passage, states that he had never seen it.

[3] *Journey to Parnassus* composed by Miguel de Cervantes Saavedra,

Nothing seems to be known of Bernardo Gonçalez de Bouadilla save what he himself tells us, that he was a native of the Canary Islands, and a student at Salamanca. The author explains his motive for writing about the Henares: " that peaceful stream, of little renown in literature for lack of knowledge in the writers. . . . .For, living by the level banks of the Tormes, where celebrated Salamanca is situated, and being a native of the famous Canary Islands, it may seem extraordinary in me to attempt to describe what my eyes have never seen. And that it may not seem a mere idle whim of mine to meddle with matters of which I have no knowledge, be it known that I was moved solely by having heard a companion of mine, a native of the famous Alcalá, bestow such praise upon its river, tell such marvelous tales of the country, so eulogize the beauty of its ladies and the courtliness and wit of its gallants, that I was naturally inclined to describe in my rude prose and ill-turned verse what my companion had related of the Summer festivities," etc.

He then sends his book into the world with the following *envoy:*

Bernardo á su Libro.

> ¡ O pobre librillo mio,
> Pues desciendes de aldeanos!
> Más te valiera en los llanos
> Apacentar tu cabrío,
> Que tratar con cortesanos.

The work, of mixed prose and verse, is divided into six books. The verse is better than the prose and is generally agreeable, easy and graceful.[1]

translated into English tercets, with preface and illustrative notes by James Y. Gibson, London, 1883, p. 143.

[1] Gallárdo, *Ensayo,* III, col. 86.   In a subsequent volume, in which

Since writing the above, I have examined the copy of the *Nymphs and Shepherds of the Henares* in the British Museum. It begins as follows:

"En las umbrosas riberas que el apacible Henares con mansas y claras olas fertiliza, andaua el pastor Florino mas cuydadoso de alimentar el fuego que en su corazon se criaua, que de apacentar su ganado por las viciosas y regaladas yeruas de los floridos prados. Pastor que en un tiempo toda su gloria tenia puesta en mirar libremente los sonorosos arroyuelos, que por entre blances guijas se derramauan: y los frondosos salzes transluzidos en la claridad de las espejadas aguas: y en oyr cantar dulcemente los paxarillos que meneando las harpadas lenguas hinchen los ayres de suaues accentos. Mas agora tiene tan mudado el gusto que sino es quando sus ojos presurosas lagrimas vierten no puede sentir rastro de alegria, por darle la fortuna no menores encuentros, que el amoroso fuego desconfianças. Siempre andaua en la consideracion de su mal excessiuo, que de dia ni de noche, le consentia un punto poder dar a sus cansados miembros algun aliuio. Viendose pues en un lugar solitario y vestido de las riquezas del alegre verano, forçado de su profundo sentimiento, de un lanudo çurron sacó un pulido instrumento y tocandole espaciosamente, esparció la voz por el ayre deste suerte:

> "Dorada aurora que con luz hermosa
> Tanto esclareces la terrena esphera,
> en ti comiença mi congoxa fiera
> a cobrar fuerza en mi serena Diosa.
> Horrida noche, obscura y tenebrosa
> de mi dolor esquiuo mensagera,
> pues mientras passas tu veloz carrera
> passo vida mas triste y mas penosa.

Gallardo again treats of our author (iv, col. 1187), he says: "although there are some well-turned verses, there are scarcely any that rise above mediocrity."

Tu, Diosa, que de gracias y grandeza
tienes a Amor un templo fabricado,
sobre cordura y virginal limpieza,
do fuerças yr el coraçon prendado
a dar la libertad a tu belleza,
tu tambien el mio has sojuzgado."

" Dando a entender que no solamente el, pero muchos y muy pulidos pastores amauan a la hermosa Roselia, la mas linda pastora que en todas aquellas riberas apacentaua ganado. Inuidiada de las bellas ciudadanas y señoras, acostumbradas a conuersar con cauallleros cortesanos. Que aunque en rusticos exercicios criada y nacida, las sobrepujaua a todas en discrecion y belleza de grande honestidad acompañada. Sus cabellos eran como el oro de Arabia en madexuelas compuesto, su blanca frente, mas luziente que el cristal, sus ojos amorosos, zarcos y modestos, la nariz proporcionada, todo su rostro quajado de blanquisima leche, sus labios vertiendo sangre, sus mexillas mas que los corales finos coloradas, las manos rollizas y de tal suerte, que parecian hechas de las sabrosas mantequillas de su aldea. No podia el rigor del Sol ardiente empecer el resplandor de su lustroso rostro, ni el pesadillo cayado exasperar sus ternissimas manos."

It will be seen that all the defects of the pastoral romance are accentuated in this work. Indeed, it would be hard to find anything more absurd than the " Nymphs and Shepherds of the Henares," and it was such books as this that brought upon the pastoral romances the ridicule with which Cervantes treats some of them.[1]

---

[1] To an interesting volume of essays by Zerolo, *Legajo de Varios,* Paris, 1897, Sr. José Maria Asensio contributes a short article on the relations between Cervantes and Gonzalez de Bouadilla, in which he conjectures that Cervantes may have been the student at Salamanca referred to above as having suggested the " Nymphs and Shepherds of the Henares" to its author. Sr. Asensio's article, however, is not convincing.

THE "SHEPHERD OF IBERIA," BY BERNARDO DE LA VEGA.

THIS romance, which appeared at Seville in 1591,[1] was likewise upon the library shelves of the famous Manchegan Knight, and it, too, was incontinently committed to the rubbish heap in the yard.[2] Nicolas Antonio tells us that Bernardo de la Vega was a native of Madrid and canon of Tucuman, an assertion that is not accepted by Clemencin.[3] I have never seen this romance, which, according to Gallardo is composed of prose and verse and is divided into four books.[4]

[1] *El Pastor de Iberia, compuesto por Bernardo de la Vega, gentil-hombre andaluz. Dirigido a D. J. Tellez Giron, Duque y Conde de Ureña, Camarero-mayor del Rey nuestro señor y su Notario mayor de los reinos de Castilla* (Escudo). Con privilegio en Sevilla, en casa de J. de Leon, impresor, 1591. A costa de Bernardo de la Vega. Gallardo, *Ensayo*, IV, col. 957.

[2] See above, p. 133.

[3] *Don Quixote*, ed. Clemencin, Vol. I, Madrid, 1833, p. 144, n. That Bernardo de la Vega had visited the Indies seems probable from another work of which he was the author: *La bella Cotalda y Cerco de Paris; Relacion de las Grandezas del Piru, Mexico y los Angeles.* Mexico, Melchor de Ocharte, 1601. 8°. Graesse, p. 270. El Canónigo Bernardo de la Vega also contributed some verses to a volume published in Mexico in 1600. Salvá, *Catálogo*, No. 351.

[4] It is thus described by Clemencin: "El lenguage es malo: se truecan los tiempos de los verbos, y se encuentran solecismos. La invencion corresponde al lenguage. El pastor Filardo, que hace el primer papel en la novela, es perseguido por sospechos de asesinato: le prende el alguacil de la aldea: se libra por el favor de dos padrinos que tiene en Sevilla: se embarca en Sanlúcar: vuélvenle á prender in Canárias: vuelve á librarle otro padrino. La pastora Marfisa, amante de Filardo, hace tantos ó más versos que su pastor: y este los hace

137

llenos de erudicion mitológica é histórica, y alegando á Platon, á Nebrija y al concílio de Trento.   Entre otras lindezas escribia Filardo á su padrino de Canárias:

> " En España passé vida tranquila
> Gozando con quietud mis verdes años
> No invidiando á Nestor ni á la Sibila."
>
> *Don Quixote,* Vol. I, p. 144, note.

Cervantes ridicules " The Shepherd of Iberia" in his " Journey to Parnassus," Book iv.   See above.

THE "ENAMORADA ELISEA" OF COVARRUBIAS.

In 1594 there appeared at Valladolid a pastoral romance entitled *La Enamorada Elisea,* by Jeronimo de Cobarrubias Herrera.[1] It is composed of five books in prose and verse, in the manner of the *Diana,* the scene being laid in Egypt, on the banks of the Nile. According to Gayangos[2] it contains some beautiful poetry, especially a dialogue between Felix and Elisea in the second book. The fourth contains five eclogues and a novel entitled " The Loves of Florisuaro and Alcida," written wholly in verse. The fifth book, which has no connection whatever with the rest of the work, is composed of canciones, glosas, octavas, sonnets, etc., and is a sort of *cancionero,* in which there are four compositions on the death of Queen Doña Ana, wife of Philip II. (1580), a reply of Abindarraez to Xarifa, written in *redondillas* and a *romance* of Rodrigo de Narvaez, which is of interest, in connection with the tale of Montemayor. It is as follows:

> En el tiempo que reinaba
> Fernando, bravo guerrero,
> Hubo un alcaide en Alora,
> Animoso caballero,

[1] *Los cinco Libros intitulados La enamorada Elisea, compuestos por Jeronimo de Cobarrubias Herrera, vecino de la villa de Medina de Rio seco, residente en Valladolid.* Dirigidos a D. Felipe II., primero rey de las Españas, nuestro Señor. Con licencia impreso en Valladolid por Luis Delgado, impresor, 1594. 8°, pp. 255. Of all the pastoral romances, this, in the opinion of Salvá, is the rarest.

[2] Ticknor, *History of Spanish Lit.,* Spanish tr., III, p. 542.

A quien llamaban Narvaez
(Rodrigo el nombre primero),
En las armas y caballo
Astuto, diestro y ligero.
Este en ganar Antequera
Se halla ser el primero
Por eso la fuerza della
Se la entrega al caballero;
Entrambas fuerzas tenia,
Por ser fiel y verdadero,
Mas habitaba en Alora
Este valiente guerrero
Con cincuenta caballeros
A sueldo del rey severo.
Pues una noche en verano,
No con la luz del lucero,
Mas con la clara Diana
Que alumbre el valle y otero,
Salió il valeroso alcaide
Con cuatro por un sendero,
Echando per otra parte
Otros cinco de su fuero,
Todos con lanzas y adargas,
Con ánimo verdadero
Van á recorrer el campo,
Por si topan caballero
Que puedan traer á Alora
Rendido por prisionero;
Entre sí van concertados
De hacerse seña primero
Si sienten gente en el campo,
Si encuentran aventurero.
Ya que llegaban los cinco
Sin el alcaide guerrero.
A vista de una emboscada,
Por debajo de un palero,
Vieron con la clara luna
Un gallardo caballero,
Y no en caballo morcillo,
Alazan, bayo ni overo,
Mas era rucio rodado,
Al parecer, muy ligero,
Con marlota de damasco
Carmesí, traje extranjero,

Borceguí, toca morisca,
Como moro verdadero.
Una lanza de los hierros,
Con una adarga de cuero,
Cantando en algarabia
Las palabras que refiero:
"En Cartama fui criado,
Nasci en Granada primero,
Tengo mi dama en Coin,
Y de Alora soy frontero."
Los cinco, que al moro vieron
Con ánimo verdadero,
Dieron sobre el fuerte moro,
Y él acometió ligero,
Tanto, que al primero encuentro
Se derrocó un caballero;
Y volviéndose á los otros,
Siguió el segundo al primero:
De suerte les apretaba,
Que lo mismo hizo al tercero.
A esta sazon los otros
Hizen señal al guerrero,
Que es Rodrigo de Narvaez,
El cual llegó muy ligero,
Y se puso rostro á rostro
Contra el enemigo fiero,
Que era dispuesto y tallado
Cual nunca se vió Rugero
En busca de Bradamante
En medio del campo fiero;
Al cual dió ciertas heridas
Y rindió por prisionero.

In general the author's versification is said to be easy and fluent; at the end of the third book he promises a second part of the Elisea, which never appeared, nor have the two comedias, which he promised, so far as I know. As is frequently the case in these pastoral romances, Gallardo says, the story in the *Enamorada Elisea* is a mere thread upon which to string a number of poems, " not sufficient to make a book, but quite enough to adorn a tale."

THE " ARCADIA " OF LOPE DE VEGA.

In 1598 Lope de Vega published his *Arcadia*.[1] Both Ticknor[2] and Schack[3] state that it was written for Lope's patron, Don Antonio of Toledo, Duke of Alba, and grandson to the great Duke of that name. This statement is evidently made upon the authority of Montalvan, who says that Lope entered the service of the Duke of Alba shortly after his return from the University of Alcalá; that the Duke not only made Lope his secretary, but also his favorite (*su valido*), a favor which Lope repaid by writing at the Duke's direction " la ingeniosa *Arcadia*," etc. This is not altogether accurate; Lope did not enter the service of the Duke of Alba till 1590, and in March, 1595, he was still attached to the household of the Duke.[4] Ticknor asserts, moreover, that the *Arcadia* was written immediately after the publication of the *Galatea* of Cervantes in 1584, which is, of course, impossible. Barrera, discrediting the above

[1] *Arcadia, Prosas y Versos de Lope de Vega Carpio, Secretario del Marques de Sarria. Con una exposicion de los nóbres Historicos, y Poeticos. A Don Pedro Tellez Giron, Duque de Osuna, &c. Con Privilegio. En Madrid, Por Luis Sanchez. Ano* 1598. 8°. The title surrounded by a border; above a scroll, with the legend: " Este Giron para el suelo, saco de su capa el cielo "; below, also in a scroll: " De Bernardo es el blason, Las desdichas mias son." There is a copy of this exceedingly rare first edition in the Ticknor library.

[2] *History of Spanish Literature*, Boston, 1888, Vol. II, p. 185.

[3] *Geschichte der dramatischen Literatur und Kunst in Spanien*, Frankfurt a. M., 1854, Vol. II, p. 166.

[4] Rennert, *Life of Lope de Vega*, Glasgow, 1904, pp. 39, 64, 98, *et passim*.

statement of Montalvan, adds: " all indications seem to prove that the *Arcadia* must have been written shortly before the year 1598, in which it first appeared in print." [1] Perhaps we can determine the date of composition a little more precisely. In fact Barrera finally fixes it between 1592 and 1596; [2] the first date being determined by a supposed reference in the *Arcadia* to the death of Lope's first wife, Doña Isabel de Urbina, which Barrera believed took place in 1592. I have shown, however, that, in all probability, Doña Isabel did not die till some time after April 22, 1595. [3] That the *Arcadia* was written while Lope was still in the service of Duke Antonio of Alba, is proved by his own words in his " Eclogue to Claudio ":

> " Siruiendo al generoso Duque Albano,
>   Escriui del *Arcadia* los Pastores,
>   Bucolicos amores
>   Ocultos siempre en vano,
>   Cuya zampoña de mis patrios lares
>   Los sauzes animó de Mançanares." [4]

There can hardly be a doubt (as had long since been pointed out by Barrera, *op. cit.,* p. 66) that the passage near the close of the *Arcadia,* entitled: " Belardo a la Çampoña," refers to the death of Doña Isabel; he speaks of the banks of the Mançanares, which he had left " to seek a new lord (*dueño*) and a new life "; and continues: " Que más vale, quando se perdió algun bien, huyr del lugar en que se tenia. . . . La fortuna llevo dudosa: pero que puede suceder mal, à quien en su vida tuuo bien? El que yo tenia perdi, más

---

[1] Barrera, *Nueva Biografia,* in *Obras de Lope de Vega* (Academy's ed.), Madrid, 1890, Vol. I, p. 42, n.

[2] *Ibid.,* pp. 65, 66.

[3] *Life of Lope de Vega,* p. 106.

[4] *La Vega del Parnaso,* Madrid, 1637, fol. 96.

porque no le merecia gozar, que porque no le supe conocer, etc. This supposition is strengthened by the epistle to Placido de Tosantos, Bishop of Oviedo, written long afterwards, and inserted in the *Circe* (written after 1619 and before 1623), in which Lope says: "After time made you a courtier and I left the Alba of Duke Antonio, my sun having suffered a human eclipse." That this is an allusion to the death of his wife is almost certain.[1]

The *Arcadia* was therefore written between 1590 and 1595. In another passage Barrera concludes that 1592-1594 is the period during which this pastoral was written.[2] While his deduction is the result of pure conjecture, there is other evidence which enables us to say with some degree of certainty that the *Arcadia* was written, or the greater part of it, at least, before 1594. It is found in a ballad which appeared in that year,[3] and in which mention is made of "the great shepherd Albano, who is grazing his flocks on the banks of the Tormes."

---

[1] See *Life of Lope de Vega,* p. 106.

[2] *Op. cit.,* p. 68. In a poem inserted in Book V. of the *Arcadia,* near the close of the work, we are told that the young Antonio (*el nueuo Antonio*) is still unmarried (p. 457, ed. of 1605); but we do not know when Don Antonio married Da. Mencia de Mendoza, daughter of the Duke of Infantado, nor do we know when their eldest son, D. Fernando Jacinto Alvarez de Toledo, Duke of Huescar was born. Sr. Barrera piles one hypothesis upon another in order to reach his conclusion, though he hits very close to the mark, as we shall see. If we knew when D. Antonio was born, all would be settled definitely, for in Book IV. we are told that he was twenty-three years old. Likewise the death of the shepherd Anfriso's (Antonio's) mother, the shepherdess Bresinda (i. e. Da. Brianda de Beaumont, Countess of Lerin, mother of the Duke Antonio) is mentioned in Book IV. But this date is also unknown to me. *Ibid.,* p. 67.

[3] In the *Sexta Parte de Flor de Romances Nuevos Recopilados de muchos Autores, por Pedro Flores, Librero.* Toledo, 1594. The *Tassa* is of July 9, 1594. In the *Prologo* to this Parte, there is a ballad,

After this long digression concerning the date of composition of the *Arcadia,* which we are unable to fix more precisely than some time between 1591 and 1594, when Lope was certainly living with his wife Doña Isabel de Urbina at Alba de Tormes, let us turn to our main purpose. The protagonist of the *Arcadia,* disguised under the name of Anfriso, is Don Antonio, Duke of Alba, and the story " relates the unhappy love affairs of this noble." The

which Ticknor conjectures upon strong evidencee, to be the work of Lope de Vega. The verses are:

* * * * *

> Junté, en nombre de Riselo,
> De Lisardo y de Belardo,
> Mil vocables pastoriles
> Bien compuestos y ordenados;
> Una amorosa porfia
> De zagal enamorado,
> Un Duque y un Conde puesto
> En abito disfraçado,
> Ora que se finge Çayde,
> Ora el gran pastor Albano
> Que en las riberas del Tormes
> Apacienta su ganado."

See Ticknor, *History of Spanish Literature,* Vol. III, p. 479. Here Belardo = Lope de Vega; Riselo = Pedro Liñan y Riaza, and Lisardo = Luis de Vargas Manrique, the two latter great friends of Lope. Lope's dedication of the *Arcadia* to " Don Pedro Tellez Giron, Duque de Osuna," also furnishes evidence as to the date of composition of that work. He says: " Al Duque, que Dios tiene, auia yo dirigido mi Arcadia, y no pudiendo imprimirla entonces," etc. The Duke to whom Lope alludes as being then deceased was Don Juan Tellez Giron, second Duke of Osuna and first Marquis de Peñafiel. According to Bethencourt, *Historia Genealogica y Heráldica de la Monarquia Española,* Madrid, 1890. Vol. II, p, 555, this Duke died November 25, 1600. That this date is impossible is shown by the *Arcadia* itself, which appeared in 1598. Rodriguez Marin, *Pedro de Espinosa,* p. 185, says that he died in 1594. This date is consonant with other known facts, and again fixes the composition of the *Arcadia* before that year. The passage " Belardo a la Campoña" was addęd, in all probability, a year or more after the work had been written.

Arcadia is clearly modeled on the ' Arcadia ' of Sannazaro. Lope tells us as much in the *Segunda Parte de las Rimas* (Madrid, 1602, fol. 243) in the dedication to Don Juan de Arguijo, where he quotes the opening sentence of Sannazaro's prologue. He justifies his imitation in these terms: " The eclogues of these shepherds are not to be found fault with because they are imitated, nor is the argument of the *Angelica* because the framework is Ariosto's,—for he likewise took it from Count Mateo Maria [Boiardo]." He does not write his *Arcadia* for the common crowd, saying: " It is not well in writing, to use expressions so unusual that they are not intelligible to anybody, for if by chance the matter be obscure those who are unlettered condemn the book, because they would have it filled with tales and novels, a thing that is unworthy of men of letters, for it is not fitting that their books should circulate among artisans and ignorant persons, for, when the object is not to teach, one should not write for those who are unable to understand." (*Ibid.*, fol. 245v.)

The *Arcadia* is a true story, Lope says (*Ibid.*, fol. 244), and it must have been primarily intended for those who could understand it. In the *prologo* he tells us that his shepherds " are not so rude that they may not, at times, rise from shepherds to courtiers, and from rustics to philosophers," and: " If, in describing another's misfortunes I have not succeeded, my excuse is that nobody can speak well in the thoughts of another; " though he admits that in this pastoral he has wept not only the misfortunes of another, but also his own.

The scene of the *Arcadia* is laid " Entre las dulces aguas del caudaloso Erimanto y el Ladon fertil, (famosos y claros rios de la pastoral Arcadia, la mas intima region del Peloponesso) . . . alli estaua el blanco Narcisso listado de oro, oloroso testigo de la filaucia, y amor propio, de aquel man-

cebo que engañó la fuente, y la rosa encarnada, que resti-
tuyó á Apuleyo en su primera forma, nacida de la sangre
de los pies de Venus, quando corriendo por las espinas, fue
á socorrer á Adonis; y la flor en que por ella fue trans-
formado no menos olorosa que su madre Myrra: y el lino
en que se conuirtio su esposo de Hypermestra, tan semejante á los que aman por sus infinitos martyrios: y tan
florido y verde, que parecia que despreciaua el lino Indiano,
que tanto admiró los antiguos, viendole resistir al fuego;
la açuzena, que tomó la Aurora del blanco seno de la Nynfa
Clorida: y la flor que fue engendrada de las lagrimas de la
Troyana Helena, tan fauorable á la hermosura de las mu-
geres, etc. . . . Por la una parte las juncosas margenes de
un pequeño braço del Erimanto fertilizauan: y por la otra
unos arroyos puros, que de una sierra baxauan de los elados
vientos del Inuierno, las espaldas le defendian. Esta eterna
habitacion de Faunos, y Amadryades, era tan celebrada de
enamorados pensamientos, que á penas en toda la espessura
se hallara tronco sin mote escrito en el liso papel de su cor-
teza tierna, porque ni el rio corrio jamas sin amorosas lagrimas, ni respondio la parlera Eco menos que á tristes
quexas: porque hasta los dulces cantos de las libres aues
repetian enternecidos sentimientos, y las indomables fieras,
con mal formados bramidos enamoradas lastimas," [1] etc.

The heroine is Belisarda, " as unhappy as she is beautiful," who loved Anfriso *castamente*. In a dream she sees
" her beloved Anfriso in the arms of another shepherdess,
who called him husband," and now she sings the following
song:

> O burlas de amor ingrato,
>   Que todas soys de una suerte,
>   Sueño, imagen de la meurte,
>   Y de la vida retrato.
> Que importa que se desuelen

[1] *Arcadia*, Anveres, 1605, p. 18.

Los interiores sentidos,
Si los de afuera dormidos
Sufrir sus engaños suelen.
Yo vi sin ojos mi dueño
En agena voluntad:
Qué pudiera la verdad
Si pudo matarme el Sueño?
Donde dormir presumi,
Descansé para mi daño,
Que el sueño de amor engaño
Me ha desengañado á mi.
Amorsosas fantasias
Sueñan alegres historias;
Yo sola en agenas glorias
Contemplo desdichas mias.
Porque con ser mis contentos
Sueño ligero y fingido;
Aun en sueños he tenido
Fingidos contentamientos.
O triste imaginacion
Para el mal siempre despierta,
Quien dira, viendo os tan cierta,
Que los sueños sueños son?
Que si no son desvarios,
Ver á Anfriso en otros braços,
Antes de tales abraços
Se bueluen laurel con mios. etc. (pp. 24-25).

Anfriso, coming through the trees, approaches Belisarda, whom he addresses in the most extravagant language, after which he makes the following vow: " The sun shall first set in the East and rise in the West, the snows of the Alps be united in peace with the flames of Aetna, or the dangers of Scylla and the Ausonian sea be joined with the shore of Sicily, ere I shall cease to be thine " (p. 29). *Aqui con un abraço honesto, ligava Belisarda el venturoso cuello del enternecido Anfriso,* when they hear Leriano and Galafron singing:

A quien yela el desden, y el amor arde,
Que sufra ingratitud à su despecho,
Por mas que en mi enemiga me acouarde

De piedra el coraçon, de nieue el pecho:
Y que en el alma sus agrauios guarde,
Reduzidos al punto mas estrecho,
Porque tarde o temprano, siempre alcança
Un largo amor justissima vengança.

Un largo amor justissima vengança
  Pide à los cielos de un ingrato oluido,
  Que ni tiene à si mismo semejança,
  Ni se parece à quanto es oy, ni ha sido:
  Todo animal que algun sentido alcança,
  Su deuda paga à amor de aquel sentido,
  Quien no conoce à amor, ni vee, ni siente,
  Llamese piedra, y huya de la gente.

While these two shepherds, both enamoured of Belisarda,
"and of unequal age, though equally abhorred," are singing, Anfriso and Belisarda drive their flocks elsewhere.
Presently they hear Isabella, who appears with Leonisa,
singing, "both of them intimate friends of Belisarda," and
with them Alcino and Menalca. The shepherd Olimpio appears singing the following sonnet:

No queda mas lustroso y cristalino
  Por altas sierras el arroyo elado,
  Ni està mas negro el euano labrado,
  Ni mas azul la flor del verde lino,
Mas rubio el oro que de Oriente vino,
  Ni mas puro, lasciuo, y regalado,
  Espira olor el ambar estimado,
  Ni està en la concha el carmesi mas fino
Que frente, cejas, ojos y cabellos,
  Aliento y boca de mi Ninfa bella,
  Angelica figura en vista humana;
Que puesto que ella se parece à ellos,
  Biuos estan alli, muertos sin ella
  Cristal, euano, lino, oro, ambar, grana [1] (p. 49).

---

[1] This summation or repetition in the last line is often employed by
Lope in his sonnets and is of especial frequency in his earlier comedias.
In this he was especially imitated by Calderon, who uses it in nearly
all his plays. Ximenez Paton in his very interesting, but I fear, much

Menalca now relates a story in the course of which these shepherdesses speak of Messalina and Semiramis, of Nero, Octavian, Seneca and Vergil. Suddenly a band of shepherds appear, including Celio, Tirsi, Amarilis, Danteo (the latter carves effigies of the shepherdesses upon the ends of their crooks),—and also *el ingenioso Benalcio, sabio Matematico*,[1] " and considered an oracle in these mountains," as well as Celso, who wrote epigrams and hung them on the trees *a honor de las Musas*. He afterwards sings about four hundred lines for the gratification of the company, the last four being:

> " Porque me dizen pastores
> Con experiencia de agrauios,
> Que sera la muerte sola
> El medico de mis daños " (p. 91).

The first book concludes with the song of Benalcio, the wise mathematician.

We are now introduced to Sylvio, " one of the most valiant shepherds of all Arcadia, feared not only by men, but by the wild boars, bears and lions." Through the treachery of Galafron, Anfriso is banished, going to the valley of " the famous Liseo." He bids farewell to his fathers " pensive, melancholy and sad," singing this sonnet:

> Excelsas torres y famosos muros,
> Cerca antigua, lustrosos chapiteles,
> Ocultos sotos, que jamas pinzeles
> Supieron retratar vuestros escuros,
> Liquidas aguas, y cristales puros,
> Dignos de Zeusis, y el diuino Apeles,
> Hermosas plantas, celebres laureles,
> De todo tiempo y tempestad seguros.

neglected *Eloquencia española* refers to this very sonnet of Lope, which he quotes. *Mercurius Trimegistus etc.*, Baeza, Pedro de la Cuesta, 1621, fol. 69.

[1] Juan Bautista Labaña?

> A Dios prendas, que un tiempo de la gloria
> (Que pensando no veros se me acorta)
> Fuistes, qual sois agora de mis daños,
> Biuid, mientras biuiere en mi memoria,
> Si ya la Parca en el partir no corta
> El tierno tronco de mis verdes años (p. 113).

There is a festival in honor of the goddess *Pales,* whose temple is hewn " out of the very bowels of the mountain," where satyrs, fauns, nymphs, hamadryads, *y otras figuras de semidioses* appear. Leriano sings a song " to jealousy," beginning :

> Nace un terrible animal
> En la prouincia sospecha,
> Mas ligero que una flecha,
> Y que un veneno mortal.
> Al amor tiene por padre,
> Y es ligitimo en rigor,
> Y con ser su padre amor,
> Tiene la embidia por madre.

After which Celsio discusses the various " *composturas* introduced into the world by women for the purpose of heightening their beauty and concealing their defects." By this time they have arrived at a cave containing the tombs of Don Gonzalo de Giron, the Marques de Santa Cruz, and the Duke of Alba, when the astrologer Benalcio recites a poem at each tomb.

The third book opens with Anfriso in his banishment reciting these beautiful lines :

> Amargas horas de los dulces dias,
> Que un tiempo la fortuna, amor, ye el cielo,
> Juntos, quisieron que gozasse el alma,
> Que agora os llora en soledades tristes,
> Qué me quereis, mostrandome memorias
> De aquellos años de mi vida alegres?
>
> Los estados mas prosperos y alegres,
> Con el ligero curso de los dias,

Qué nos suelen dexar sino memorias?
Todo es mudable quanto cubre el cielo,
En todo vengo à hallar memorias tristes,
Pena del cuerpo, y confusion del alma.
*   *   *   *   *   *   *

Passo mis años en discursos tristes,
Por la inclemencia del contrario cielo,
Haziendo noches los hermosos días,
Ciego el entendimiento, luz del alma,
En cuya essencia imagenes alegres
Me representan miseras memorias.

O ausencia, madre inutil de memorias,
Que asi condenas los sentidos tristes
A dessear las que gozaua alegres;
Quando lo quiso el disponer del cielo,
La vida, el gusto, el coraçon, el alma
En el plazer de aquellos breues dias.

La edad es flor, qual sombra son los dias,
Presto se desuanecen sus memorias.
O vida, en fin mortal carcel del alma,
Qué largos muestras los pesares tristes!
Mas bien podia con mudarse el cielo,
Mudar estas fortunas en alegres (p. 177).

He then draws Belisarda's portrait from his scrip, reading:

Ojos que sin luzes veis,
Boca que sin lengua hablais,
¿ Cómo sin alma escuchais,
Y sin sentido entendeis?

Lealdo and Floro arrive from Monte Menalo, saying
that Belisarda had gone to Cilena, whither Anfriso goes
disguised and meets Belisarda. Again the shepherds arrive at a cave containing marble statues of heroes and great
worthies, which are explained by the sage, always present
on such occasions. There is plenty of verse,—a stanza to
each of the statues, which include Romulus, Remus, Ly-
curgus, Alexander, Hannibal, Cæsar, Charlemagne, Cleo-
patra, Semiramis, Zenobia, Bernardo del Carpio, the Cid,

Alonso Perez de Guzman, Charles V., Fernan Cortes, the Duke of Alba and others. A sonnet follows by Belisarda:

> De verdes mantos las cortezas cubre
>   El matizado Abril de aquestas plantas,
>   De varias flores, y de frutas tantas
>   Mayo vistoso la sazon descubre.
> Junio, que de la tierra nada encubre,
>   La frente ciñe con espigas santas
>   Y por las vides con mojadas plantas
>   Negros razimos el desnudo Otubre.
> Componese de flores el mançano
>   Que puso el labrador en confiança
>   Que espere à tiempo fertiles despojos.
> Todo lo que sembró trabajo humano
>   Rinde su fruto al fin, y la esperañça
>   Tras tantos años me produze enojos (p. 231).

Anfriso, becoming jealous of Olimpio, returns to his home, where he is scarcely recognized, so greatly has he changed. He now bestows his affections upon Anarda, afterwards, however, he begins to doubt that Belisarda loves Olimpio. On seeing Anfriso weep one day, Belisarda says: What are you weeping about? Yesterday laughing with Anarda, and to-day weeping with me? What means this feigned fondness? Whom dost thou hope to deceive here, who may not know you? Belisarda leaves him, reciting some verses, beginning:

> "Dueño de mis ojos,
>   Mientras tienen lumbre,
>   Pues soy tus despojos,
>   Por gusto y costumbre,
> El alma te dexo,
>   Que el cuerpo no es mio,
>   Y míentras me alexo,
>   Suspiros te embio.
> Injustas venganças
>   Mataron mis dichas,
>   Fingidas mudanças
>   Fueron mis desdichas.

Quien no piensa y mira
  Primero que intente,
  En vano suspira,
  Tarde se arrepiente.
*   *   *   *   *

Tuya fue la culpa,
  Yo tengo la pena,
  Tardia disculpa
  Para nada es buena.
*   *   *   *   *

Casada y cansada
  Estoy de un dia,
Amando pagada,
  Quando no soy mia.
Pero eternamente
  Mi dueño te nombra,
  Que el tirano ausente
  Servira de sombra.
*   *   *   *   *

Tan aborrecida
  Estoy de perderte,
  Que temo la vida,
  Y adoro la muerte " (p. 387).

To which Anfriso replies with the following *romance:*

Hermosissima pastora,
Señora de mi aluedrio,
Reyna de mis pensamientos,
Esfera de mis sentidos.
Cielo del alma que os doy,
Sol que adoro, luz que miro,
Fenix de quien soy el fuego,
Dueño de quien soy cautivo ;
Regalo de mi memoria,
Retrato del parayso,
Alma de mi entendimiento,
Y entendimiento diuino.
Hermosa señora, Reyna,
Esfera, cielo, Sol mio,
Luz, Fenix, dueño, regalo,
Imagen, alma, y auiso ;
Si os he ofendido,
Matenme zelos, y en ausencia oluido.

> Embidias me den la muerte,
> Vengando à mis enemigos,
> Con las armas encubiertas,
> Y voz de amigos fingidos.
> Mi propia sangre me engañe,
> Mis quexas no hallen oydos,
> Mis suspiros os den pena,
> Y mis memorias oluido.
> Trayciones me desengañen,
> Zelos me quiten el juyzio,
> Pensamientos el sustento,
> Desuarios el sentido, etc. (p. 389).

In the Fifth Book the shepherds are led by the wise Polinesta to an immense temple, "much larger than that of Diana and Apollo," where they see a beautiful maiden teaching youths. She recites dull poems on Grammar, Logic, Rhetoric, Astrology, Music, Poetry, etc. Hanging in the halls they see portraits of the Duke of Sessa, Diego de Mendoza, *el divino* Garcilasso, *el cortesano* Boscan, etc. "And now, it seems to me, said the venerable sage, that you, Anfriso, are prepared to go to the sacred temple of enlightenment," etc. (*templo del desengaño*). Let us go, said Anfriso, for there is nothing that I desire so anxiously, for if it were not to leave you suspicious, I believe that I would ask you who you are, for of my *enemiga* (Belisarda) already I scarcely remember the name. Frondoso and Polinesta, as was just, laughed at this apathy (*descuido*), Anfriso concluding with the poem beginning:

> La verde Primauera
> De mis floridos años
> Passé cautiuo, amor, en tus prisiones:
> Y en la cadena fiera,
> Cantando mis engaños,
> Lloré con mi razon tus sinrazones;
> Amargas confusiones
> Del tiempo, que has tenido
> Ciega mi alma, y loco mi sentido.

The last stanza:

> Quede por las cortezas
> De aquestos verdes arboles,
> Ingrata fiera, con mi fe tu nombre
> Imprima en las durezas
> De aquestos blancos marmoles
> Mi exemplo amor, que à todo el mundo assombre,
> Y sepase que un hombre
> Tan ciego y tan perdido,
> Su vida escriue, y llora arrepentido (p. 469).

A dictionary of poetical and historical names, consisting of fifty-eight double-column pages, with which the work concludes, will give an idea of the learning with which it is crowded.

The *Arcadia* of Lope de Vega, however, despite this ostentation of learning, its great length and its flowery and extravagant diction, was very successful. It did not escape the metaphysical discussions with which its predecessors were burdened, nor could it claim much merit on the score of originality and invention, as it followed pretty closely in the beaten track, and where all was hopelessly involved, the *deus ex machina,* the convenient sorceress, was called in, who, by some mysterious means, brought about the desired end. The pastoral tone, however, is almost entirely sacrificed and the story is wanting in truth to nature; a number of episodes are introduced that have no connection with what either precedes or follows, and in at least two instances, for the sole purpose of praising the house of his patron. Its poetry, however, already shows the great master, containing, in fact, all the peculiarities of his later manner: the extravagant hyperboles, the peculiar repetition of the thought in another form (afterward imitated by Calderon, as already observed), the easy and graceful versification,— all are already here.[1]   —

---

[1] It may be noted here that Lope closes his romance with the address: *Belardo à la çampoña,* just as Sannazaro, his acknowledged model, ends his *Arcadia.*

THE "PRADO OF VALENCIA" BY D. GASPAR MERCADER.

In 1600 a pastoral romance entitled *The Prado of Valencia* by D. Gaspar Mercader, Count of Buñol, appeared at Valencia.[1] Its author was born at Valencia, in 1567, the son of Gaspar Mercader, Count of Buñol, and Doña Laudomia Carroz. In 1583 Don Gaspar, the younger, married Da. Hipólita Centellas, both being under sixteen years of age. They occupied a prominent position in the society of their native city. In 1592 Mercader became a member of the *Academia de los Nocturnos,* to which Guillen de Castro, Tárrega, Aguilar and all the principal Valencian peots belonged.[2] In this Academy he assumed the name *Relámpago*. He was a man of wild, unbridled temper, and in 1593, in the streets of Valencia, he killed a wretched, half-witted man who had pulled the tail of his horse, first running him through with his sword and then cutting off his head, though the poor fellow lay on the ground and im-

---

[1] *El Prado de Valencia. Compuesto por Don Gaspar Mercader. A la Illustrissima y Excellentissima señora Doña Calalina de la Cerda y Sandoual, Duquessa de Lerma, Marquesa de Denia, y Sea, Condessa de Empudia, y Camarera mayor de la Reyna nuestra Señora* [device]. En Valencia, por Pedro Patricio Mey, MDC. It again issued from the same press in the following year. It was not reprinted until 1907, when an excellent critical edition, with introduction and notes by Henri Mérimée, appeared at Toulouse. It is to this edition that I am indebted for the facts of Mercader's life.

[2] The *Cancionero* of this literary Academy, the manuscript of which was formerly in the possession of the bibliographer D. Pedro Salvá and afterward became the property of the Biblioteca Nacional, was published in 1905-06. I possess one of the copies of this edition of twenty-five. It is entitled: *Cancionero de la Academia de los Nocturnos de Valencia, estractado de sus actas originales por D. Pedro Salvá y reimpreso con adiciones y notas de Francisco Martí Grajales* [device]. Valencia, MCMV.

plored his mercy. For this murder Mercader was never punished. He died August 7, 1631.

The work takes its name, the *Prado de Valencia,* from a flowery promenade which existed at the close of the sixteenth century, on the left bank of the Turia, opposite the city of Valencia, on the site of the present *Alameda.* The book is a picture of manners under a pastoral disguise and in the opinion of M. Mérimée can hardly be classed among the pastoral romances, as the author, in adopting the pastoral fiction, was merely providing a convenient means of accomplishing his main purpose, which was to produce an anthology of the best poetry of the Valencian school in a prose setting of his own. This being his object, it must be admitted that he has shown great ingenuity in the construction of the work. As none of the verses had been originally written for such a purpose, it required no little skill to embody them in the intrigue of a romance. In this, however, through his eagerness to include as much of the poetry of his friends as possible, he has not always been successful, in spite of his unquestioned skill. In the words of M. Mérimée, " la *Prado de Valencia* n'est pas un recueil poétique original, c'est une anthologie." He has, moreover, succeeded in recognizing beneath their pastoral disguise, a number of well-known names. The protagonist, Fideno, is D. Gaspar Mercader himself, while Belisa is Da. Catalina de la Cerda y Sandoval, who, on November 6, 1598, married in Madrid D. Pedro Fernandez de Castro Andrade y Portugal, Count of Lemos and Marquis of Sarriá, while Lisardo may, possibly, be Don Guillen de Castro.

Although the prose of the *Prado de Valencia* is easy and fluent, there are scarcely any descriptions of natural scenery and the work is of value only on account of the poetry it contains, in which all the more celebrated *ingenios* of the Valencian school are represented.

SOLORZENO—"THE TRAGEDIES OF LOVE."

In 1607 there appeared at Madrid the "Tragedies of Love" by Juan Arze Solorzeno.[1] He was born at Valladolid in 1576, and in his *Dedicatoria* refers to this work as "these rustic thoughts, the first fruits of my tender years, brought forth when I was nineteen years old (*estos rusticos pensamientos, primicias de mis tiernos años, engendrados en los diez y nueve de mi edad*); and in his address to the Reader says that he is then not yet twenty-eight years old (the *suma de Privilegio* is dated 1604), and that in his early youth he wrote fifteen eclogues, of which he now offers the first five, saying further: "receive them well, if you would see the remaining ones."[2]

The book is best described in the author's own words: "Avendo en estas eglogas con artificiosas historias, antiguas fabulas, filiosoficos discursos, latinas y griegas inmi-

---

[1] *Tragedias de Amor, de Gustoso y Apacible Entretenimiento de Historias, Fabulas enredados Marañas, Cantares, Bayles, ingeniosas Moralidades del enamorado Acrisio, y su Zagala Lucidora. Compuesto por el Licenciado Juan Arze Solorzeno. Dirigido a Don Pedro Fernandez de Castro, Conde de Lemos, etc. Con Privilegio. En Madrid, Por Juan de la Cuesta. Año MDCVII.* 196 leaves. Gallardo (*Ensayo*, I, p. 264) mentions an edition printed at Zaragoza in 1647. Besides the "Tragedies of Love," Solorzeno is the author of the *Historia euangelica de la Vida, Milagros y Muerte de Christo, nuestro Dios y Maestro*. Madrid, 1605. Pérez Pastor, *Bibliografía Madrileña*, II, p. 83. He also translated the following work: *Historia de los dos Soldados de Christo, Barlaan y Iosafat. Escrita por san Juan Damasceno, Doctor de la Yglesia Griega. . . .* Madrid, MDCVIII.

[2] Though the privilege to print the "Tragedies of Love" is dated 1604, the author probably sought in vain, for some time, to find a publisher. On February 28, 1607, we learn that the Licentiate Arce Solorzeno, Secretary of the Bishop of Cordoba, sold the MS. and privilege of the *Primera Parte de las Traxedias de Amor* to Antonio Rodriguez, book-seller, for three hundred and fifty reals. Peréz Pastor, *Bibl. Madrileña*, II, pp. 119-120.

taciones dado alguna parte de dulce, puse al fin de cada una su breve allegoria," etc. This "allegorical interpretation" is the dullest and most insipid part of what is certainly a very dull book.

The first eclogue begins as follows:

"Rumor confuso, y clamor desordenado, de albogues, orlos, y flautos, con son funesto, y temeroso acento, en los bosques y valle resonava, quando el ingenioso Acrisio, pastor montañes gallardo (recien venido à aquella fertil ribera, y en ella tan enamorado de la bella Lucidora que fue digno de hõrosa corona de sagrado Mirto) baxaua por la fresca orilla del Sil, caudaloso rio, à tiempo que el roxo dios calentando el Signo de Leon en el dia consagrado à su triforme hermana, matizava los montes de aljofaradas listas," etc. Here is an excerpt from fol. 100. The shepherds visit the tower of Fame:

"A la qual subieron por una larga escalera en caracol, hasta llegar a la sala de la inmortalidad, que era en figura de pyramide, que començava en ancho, y yua enangostandose hasta acabar en un espacio redondo de treynta pies de circunferencia, en el qual auia un teatro de plata fina, y subiase a el por siete escalones de Jaspe leonado y blanco, y encima estaua un trono preciosissimo, pero cubierto con un gran velo de raro carmesi.

"El suelo estaua ladrillado de marfil, y euano el techo, y paredes cubiertas de laminas, florones y labores marauillosos, hechos de pieças de oro, plata, cristal, y aljofares: y en la cupula del techo auia entre quatro esmeraldas un Apyroto, que priuaua de vista al que en el ponia los ojos, y de la una parte y otra muchas estatuas de plata fina de valerosos hombres armados, de altura de ocho pies geometricos cada una, y en medio dellas, y de la sala una altra coluna de cristal, sobre la qual estatua la ligera fama, cubierta de ojos y bocas, lenguas y plumas, y a sus pies un quadro de marfil, y escrito en el con letras de oro este arrogante blason:

> La fama soy, que contra el tiẽpo, y muerte
> Y a pesar de la inuidia, y del oluido
> Doy vida eterna, y nombre esclarecido
> Al varon virtuoso, sabio, o fuerte
> (Por quien se vera el mundo enriq̃zido)
> Estoy ganando mi valor perdido,
> Y assi mi canto a ellos se conuierte.
> Ved pues, de quan illustre y noble gente
> Espero renacer en dulce canto,
> Pero passadlos todo uno a uno,
> Hasta los tres que estan ultimamente,
> Que me diran los tres que dezir tanto
> Que jamas dire mas de otro ninguno.

Among these silver statues, which are now described, the first is *Crastino,* a valiant captain, who, following Caesar's faction, hurled the first lance " *contra el campo de Pompeyo en la guerra Farsalica,*" etc.; then follow the counts of Castile, Fernan Laynez, Ruy Fernandez, and Fernan Ruyz de Castro, etc. On page 103 is told the tragic story of Fernan Ruyz de Castro and his wife Estefania (daughter of the Emperor Alfonso VII.) which is the only interesting episode in the book.[1] This is followed by a long genealogy and eulogy of the house of Castro. Mythological deities are scattered plentifully throughout the book, which concludes with a long dictionary of names, and is, upon the whole, by far the dullest of all these romances.

---

[1] This story, believed by some to be historical, is the basis of Lope de Vega's tragicomedia *La desdichada Estefania, Comedias,* Part XII, Madrid, 1619. Menéndez y Pelayo believes Lope's source to be the *Cronica de D. Alonso VII.* by Prudencio de Sandoval, Madrid, 1600, or possibly the above tale of Solorzeno. The same tragic episode was again dramatized by Luis Velez de Guevara in his play *Los Celos hasta los Cielos y desdichada Estefania.* See *Obras de Lope de Vega,* edition of the Spanish Academy, Vol. VIII, p. lxvi. Menéndez y Pelayo calls attention to the similarity of the third act of Lope's play and Shakespeare's *Othello.*

BALBUENA—"THE GOLDEN AGE."

In the following year " The Golden Age in the Forests of Erifile " appeared, being first published at Madrid, in 1608.[1] Its author, Don Bernardo de Balbuena, afterward became Bishop of Porto-Rico, and for the few known incidents of his life we are chiefly indebted to the introduction to the edition published in 1821 by the Spanish Academy,[2]

---

[1] *Siglo de Oro, en las Selvas de Erifile del Dotor Bernardo de Balbuena. En que se descrive una agradable y rigurosa imitacion del Estilo pastoril de Teocrito, Virgilio, y Sanazaro. Dirigido al Excelentissimo Don Pedro Fernandez de Castro, Côde de Lemos, y de Andrade, Marques de Sarria, y Presidente del Real Consejo de Indias.* Año 1608. *Con Privilegio. En Madrid, Por Alonso Martin. A costa de Alonso Perez, Mercader de libros.* Small 12°. Fifteen preliminary leaves and one blank; the text on pp. 9 to 165. Colophon: En Madrid. En casa de Alonso Martin. Año 1607. I possess a copy of this very rare book. On pages 1-7 there is an *Epistola al Lector* which is not noted in the bibliographical works that I have consulted. Though beginning at the top of page 1, it is not complete, as the page begins in the middle of a sentence. Apparently the author of this *Epistola* is unknown; it is certainly not Balbuena. He informs us that the writing of eclogues in mixed prose and verse was chosen by Doctor Balbuena in imitation of Sannazaro, while he has also followed Theocritus, inasmuch as the eclogues are free of any allegorical meaning, but that Balbuena also wished to imitate Vergil in preserving the decorum of the persons introduced into his eclogues, etc. He justifies the prose style of Balbuena "which may seem affected to some, 'a poetical prose,'" as he calls it, and says that the reason why the prose of Sannazaro has been called affected is because it is flowery and adorned with epithets, etc. In his dedication Balbuena says that his eclogues *en el verano de mi niñez, a bueltas de su nueuo mûdo fueron naciendo.*

[2] It should be remembered, however, that the information furnished

162

for which most of the facts were furnished by Balbuena's *Grandeza Mejicana,* a descriptive poem in eight cantos, first published in Mexico in 1604.

Bernardo de Balbuena was born in Valdepeñas on November 22, 1568; his parents, Don Gregorio Villanueua and Doña Luisa de Balbuena, both descendants of noble families that were well known for having long exercised high offices in that city. Very little is known of his early life, save that, as he himself says, he studied the humanities in one of the colleges of Mexico and gained prizes in three poetical contests,—in one instance over three hundred competitors,—when only seventeen years old.[1] He probably sailed for Spain shortly after this time (1585), to complete his studies. He seems to have been a diligent student, and became a Bachelor of Theology in the University of Mexico and Doctor in Sigüenza, one of the smaller universities of Spain. We have no further information whatever concerning Balbuena until 1603, when he was again in Mexico, and dated the dedication of his *Grandeza Mejicana* from that city.

by this edition adds nothing to the account of Balbuena given by Dieze, *Geschichte der Spanischen Dichtkunst,* Göttingen, 1769. I have been unable to discover who the editor of this second edition is.

[1] These *justas literarias* were then very common in Spain, and, probably, also in America. In Spain *justas* were held in 1595, 1608, 1614 and 1620, in which the greatest Spanish poets competed. See the *Justa poetica, y alabanzas Justas que hizo Madrid en las Fiestas de San Isidro.* Small 4°. Madrid. My copy is without date, but it is given as 1620 in the *Tassa.* Upon this occasion Lope de Vega was the judge who distributed the prizes and recited the introductory verses. See also Suarez de Figueroa, *El Passagero,* Madrid, 1617 (fol. 118), who says that " at such joustings there were more poets than sands upon the sea-shore." Figueroa was a competitor in one of these *fiestas* held at Toledo that very year (1617). See Ticknor, *History of Spanish Lit.* Spanish tr., Vol. III, p. 528. The opinion of Cervantes upon these tournaments is given in *Don Quixote,* Part II, Chap. xviii. He had gained the first prize at one held in Zaragoza in 1595.

At the age of thirty-nine (1607) he was named abbot of Jamaica, where he lived until 1620, when he was made Bishop of Porto Rico. From documents in the archives of Seville, it is known that he was present at the provincial Council of Santo Domingo in 1622 and 1623. He died on October 11, 1627,[1] in Porto Rico.

The " Golden Age "[2] is divided into twelve " eclogues " of mixed prose and verse, and though its brevity is greatly in its favor, when compared with other works of the same class, it appears never to have enjoyed much success. No edition was published between the first, in 1608, and that of 1821. It was, however, highly praised by some contemporary poets.[3]

---

[1] Balbuena also published: *El Bernardo, o la Victoria de Ronces-valles,* Madrid, 1624. I have a reprint in three volumes, dated Madrid, 1808. 12mo.

[2] While the "Golden Age" was not published till 1608, it was evidently ready for the press four years before, as the *Aprouacion,* signed by Tomas Gracian Dantisco, is dated at Valladolid, August 2, 1604. On September 10, 1607, in Madrid, Balbuena, who is described as "clerigo presbitero, residente en esta corte," sold and transferred to Alonso Perez, book-seller, all his rights and title in the royal privilege that had been granted him to print the "Golden Age," for one hundred and fifty copies of the printed book. See Pérez Pastor, *Bibliografía Madrileña,* Vol. II, p. 131. A brief, but good account of Balbuena and his works is given by Dieze, *Geschichte der Spanischen Dichtkunst,* Göttingen, 1769, p. 390.

[3] Lope de Vega praises Balbuena in his *Laurel de Apolo* (1630), saying:

> Y siempre dulce tu memoria sea,
> Generoso prelado
> Doctissimo Bernardo de Balbuena,
> Tenias tu el cayado
> De Puerto Rico, quando el fiero Enrique
> Olandes rebelado
> Robó tu libreria;
> Pero tu ingenio no, que no podia,
> Aunque las fuerças del oluido aplique.

The scene of the "Golden Age" is laid in a valley watered by the Guadiana. Among the things there most worthy to be celebrated, the author says, one, above all is "the extraordinary beauty of a clear and limpid little fountain which with its sweet waters bathes the better part of a valley, and which is known by the beloved name of Erífile." There is so much sameness in respect to incident, however, in all these works that it would be useless to chronicle the sufferings and vicissitudes of Filis and Galatea, of Delicio and Clarenio, and of the various other shepherds and shepherdesses, who were nearly always unfortunate enough to love some one by whom they were not loved in return. But the book is very much better than many that were more esteemed, and if its prose sometimes bears signs of affectation, it is often very graceful and flowing, as the following excerpts show:

"Todos en torno de la cristalina fuente nos sentamos, gozando las maravillas que en el tendido llano se mostrauan, y lo que sobre todo mayor deleyte ponia era el agradable ruydo con que los altiuos alamos, siluando en ellos un delgado viento, sobre nuestras cabeças se mouian, quajados sus tembladores ramos de pintadas avezillas, que con sus no aprendidos cantares trabajauan de remedar los nuestros, donde la solitaria tortolilla con tristes arrullos vieras llorar su perdida compañia, o al amoroso Ruyseñor recontar la no

> Que bien cantaste el Español Bernardo,
> Que bien al Siglo de Oro,
> Tu fuiste su prelado, y su tesoro,
> Y tesoro tan rico en Puerto Rico,
> Que nunca Puerto Rico fue tan rico" (fol. 13b).

Likewise Cervantes, in his *Viage al Parnaso* (ed. of 1614, Chap. iii, p. 16),

> "Este es aquel Poeta memorando,
> Que mostró de su ingenio la agudeza
> En las Selvas de Erífile cantando."

oluidada injuria del fementido Tereo, aqui el ronco Faysan sonaua, alli las suaues calandrias se oyan, aculla cantaban los çorçales, las mirlas y las abubillas, y hasta las industriosas abejas a nuestras espaldas con blando susurrar, de una florecilla en otra yuan saltando; todo olia a verano, todo prometia un año fertil y abundoso: olia el romero, el tomillo, las rosas, el açahar y los preciosos jazmines: olian las tiernas manças y las amarillas ciruelas, de que todo el campo estaba quajado; los ramos, que apenas podian sustentar la demasiada carga de su fruta, y nosotros entre tanta diuersidad de frescuras todo lo gozauamos, y por todo dauamos gracias a su diuino hazedor " (fol. 155, ed. 1608).

" De tanta suauidad fueron los versos de los Pastores, y con el silencio de la noche tan agradables de oyr, que unos vencidos de su dulçura, se quedaron en el sosegado sueño sepultados, y otros leuantando los espiritus a contemplaciones mas altas, alabaron las celestiales lumbres que puestas por testigos de nuestras vidas con resplandecientes ojos, consideran los secretos de la noche que en aquella sazon con tan agradable buelo pasaua, que si en nuestros mortales oydos cupiera semejante gloria, entonces mejor que nunca pudieramos oyr los diuinos cantos de las estrellas, si es verdad que tambien como las demas cosas ellas en medio de nuestra quietud alaban con doradas lenguas la fuente, de adonde su hermosura nace, mas luego que las alegres luzes del Alua restituyeron al mundo su alegria, y en el Oriente se declaró la mañana tan resplandeciente y bella, que no sé si de las rosas tomaua su hermoso color ó a ellas su mucha frescura se lo daua, dexando los pagizos lechos," etc. (fol. 166v).

Balbuena excels in his descriptions of nature; in this respect he surpasses all other Spanish writers of pastoral romances. As examples of his poetry, I copy the following:

Sonnet.

Hebras del oro que el Oriente embia
  Tras el rosado carro de la Aurora,
  Lazos donde enredada mi alma mora
  Cautiua con cadenas de alegria.
Rayos de luz de quien la toma el dia
  Soles con que el del cielo se desdora,
  Tesoros do la gloria se atesora,
  Que en ricas minas del amor se cria.
Ambar, madexas de oro, lazos bellos,
  Lumbres del cielo, rayos de la vida,
  Luzes del alba, flechas amorosas,
Nombres proprios son vuestros, mis cabellos,
  Sacados de la gloria, que escondida
  Está entre aquessas redes milagrosas (fol. 54v).

It is, however, only from his eclogues that we can form a just conception of the genius of Balbuena. They have been pronounced second only to those of Garcilasso de la Vega. It is inexplicable how a work containing verses of such surpassing merit, should not have been more favorably received, while greatly inferior romances passed through edition after edition. The rustic simplicity that pervades these eclogues imparts to the " Golden Age " a naturalness that is almost entirely wanting in works of this class. Balbuena's shepherds are, at least, real shepherds, not the visionary creatures with which other pastoral romances are peopled.[1] The following verses are from Eclogue V.:

Yo, seluas, cantaré las milagrosas
  Palabras que pudieran darme vida
  A ser mis penas menos poderosas.
Ya que de entera luz toda vestida

---

[1] Beraldo's song (fol. 12v), as was long since pointed out by the editor of the Madrid edition of 1821, is a paraphrase of Petrarch's famous " *Chiare, fresche e dolci acque.*" Balbuena's verses are of remarkable beauty.

La luna sobre el mundo se descubre
En purissimas llamas encendida.
Aqui donde con negra sombra encubre
La noche en sueño, y lutos sepultada,
La casta yerua que estas aras cubre;
Primero una cordera degollada
Con lumbre de laurel, y açufre puro
Al silencio sera sacrificada.
De aqui començara nuestro conjuro,
Ya aqui no ay que esperar sino la muerte,
El encanto es aqui lo mas seguro.
Y porque tu con animo mas fuerte
A semejantes cosas te apercibas,
Atento aora mi cantar aduierte.
De un negro rio aqui las aguas viuas
Tengo guardadas para que con ellas
Ciertas palabras en mi sombra escriuas,
De que seran testigos las estrellas,
Y la noche que oyendo esta su canto,
Y la luna tambien que buela entrellas.
Y porque no te cieguen con espanto
Las sombras de los dioses que vinieren,
Forçados del apremio de mi encanto.
Assi los que del ayre decendieren,
Como los que en sepulcros escondidos,
Estan siempre escuchando a los que mueren,
Con esta yerua claros y lucidos
Te dexare los ojos, que con ellos
Podras aun conocer los no nacidos.

*　　*　　*　　*　　*　　*　　*　　*

Luego do el agua sin correr se muda,
Bañado nueue vezes de mi mano,
Con la rayz de la encantada ruda.
Seguro cogeras por este llano
Las yeruas de virtud no conocida,
Que en el nacieron su primer verano, etc. (fol. 90).

The following *tercetos* are from Eclogue IV. (fol. 73).

Clarenio.	Dulce es el fresco humor a los sembrados,
	Y al ganado es la sombra deleytosa,
	Y mas Tirrena a todos mis cuydados.
Delicio.	Abre el clabel, desplegase la rosa,

Brota el jazmin, y nace la açucena,
En dando luz los ojos de mi diosa.

Clarenio. Si su beldad esconde mi Tirrena,
El jazmin cae, el açucena muere
Quando de mas frescor y aljofar llena.

Delicio. Haz tu que el sol de Filis reberbere,
Y veras que el inuierno desabrido
Con el florido Abril competir quiere.

Clarenio. Vistase de mil flores el exido,
Que se mi sol no abriere la mañana,
Todo queda en espinas conuertido.

Delicio. Mas bella es mi Tirrena, y mas loçana
Que las blancas ouejas de Taranto,
Y de arbol fertil la primer mançana.

Clarenio. Fresca es la fuente entre el florido acanto,
De rosas y violetas coronada
Y mas es la pastora que yo canto.

Delicio. O si mi Galatea enamorada
Oyera aqui mi canto y sus primores,
Como fuera rendida y obligada!

Clarenio. Frescas guirnaldas de tempranas flores,
Ninfas, coronaran uestros altares,
Si propicias guiays nuestros amores, etc.

From Eclogue VIII (fol. 121v).

Nace el inuierno, y a las tiernas rosas
Sucede un cierço que con soplo elado
Desnudo dexa el campo de frescura.
Mueren secas las flores en el prado,
Ni queda en las riberas mas umbrosas
Rastro de su passada hermosura.
Y mientras esto dura
Y con la blanca nieue
Toda la sierra llueue
Arroyos sin sazon a la llanura,
Ni suena caramillo, ni ay quien diga
En tonos de dulçura
Primores o querellas de su amiga,
Tambien quien viere el campo desta suerte
Apenas quedara con esperança
De verlo en su passada primauera.
En todo imprime el tiempo su mudança,

Y todo tiene fin sino esta muerte
En que Tirrena gusta que yo muera,
Nadie está de manera
Que una ocasion cumplida
No le dé nueua vida,
O mas dichosa, o menos lastimera,
Ni aura tan desterrado peregrino
Que no halle siquiera
Donde sentarse al fin de su camino, etc.

"THE CONSTANT AMARILIS" OF FIGUEROA.

The *Constante Amarilis* of Christoval Suarez de Figueroa was the next pastoral romance to make its appearance.[1] It was first published at Valencia in 1609. Its author was born at Valladolid, in all probability in 1572.[2] Nearly all that is known of his life he tells us in a work entitled " The Traveller,"[3] a series of ten discussions be-

---

[1] *La Constante Amarilis. Prosas y Versos de Christoval Suarez de Figueroa. Diuididos en quatro Discursos. A Don Vincencio Guerrero Marques de Montebelo, Cauallero del habito de Alcantara, Gentil hombre de la Camara del Duque de Mantua, y su Cavallerizo mayor* [device]. *Con licencia, y Privilegio. Impresso en Valencia, junto al molino de Rouella Año mil 600, y neuve.* 12°, pp. 282. I have a copy of this very rare work, also of the French translation: *La Constante Amarilis De Christoval Suarez de Figueroa. En Quatre Discours. Traduite d'Espagnol en François par N. L*[ancelot]. *Parisien. A Lyon, par Claude Morillon,* 1614, 8°, pp. 565, and index. The Spanish and French texts are on opposite pages. No other edition appeared until that of Madrid, Sancha, 1781.

[2] In Figueroa's work *Varias Noticias importantes a la humana Comunicacion,* Madrid, 1621, fol. 213, the author says that he had left his native country thirty-two years before, to travel in foreign lands; in his *Passagero,* Madrid, 1618, fol. 214, he says that he left his home at the age of sixteen. As the first-named work was written in 1620, it would give us the year 1572. See Crawford, *The Life and Works of Christoval Suarez de Figueroa,* Philadelphia, 1907, an excellent work, containing much documentary material from the archives at Naples. In 1892 I published a number of documents from MSS. in the Biblioteca Nacional, which are of considerable importance for the period 1624-30. See *Some Documents in the Life of Christoval Suarez de Figueroa,* Modern Lang. Notes, Vol. VII, pp. 398-410.

[3] *El Passagero. Advertencias utilíssimas á la Vida humana.* Madrid, Luys Sanchez, 1617.

171

tween four travelers journeying to Italy. In this autobiography, in which is mingled much that is purely fictitious, he tells us that his father was a Galician jurist, not
overburdened with this world's goods, for in the words of
the son: " he brought with him from Coruña nothing but
his cleverness," and that he removed to Valladolid to practice his profession. Figueroa tells us, moreover, that he
had a brother, and that both sons studied *Gramatica,* that is,
Latin. At the age of sixteen, envious of his brother, who,
being in poor health, was favored by his father, he resolved
to go to Italy, and declared in the presence of his parents
that he would never return to Spain during their life-time,
—a resolution which he afterwards kept. He now went to
Barcelona, thence to Genoa, thence to Milan, undecided
whether to follow the profession of arms or letters. He
finally resolved to study at Bologna or Pavia. It was
probably at the latter university that he took his doctor's
degree, *en ambos derechos.* In 1591 he entered the service
of D. Juan Hernandez de Velasco, Duke of Frias,[1] who
was then Governor of Milan, and afterwards served as
Auditor of the Spanish troops in Piedmont against the
French. It is not known how long he was occupied in this
capacity, but he was present at the final capture of the
castle of Cavour in 1595,[2] after which he returned to Milan.
In 1600 we find him as Naples, for in that year he was on
board a vessel that touched at the Barbary coast.[3] At this

[1] Crawford, *op. cit.,* p. 14.

[2] *Ibid.,* p. 15.

[3] *Varias Noticias,* etc., fol. 38. It was while living in Naples in
1602 that he is said to have published the first of the long series of
works that made his name known, a translation of the *Pastor fido* of
Guarini. Of this translation, Ticknor, *History of Spanish Literature,*
Vol. III, p. 104, note, says: " It was printed, I believe, at Naples in
1602, but was improved in the edition at Valencia in 1609." This
edition of 1602 is thus described by Salvá (*Catálogo,* I, p. 447): *El*

time his mother and brother died. He tells us that his parents often wrote to him, asking him to return, but that he always refused; afterwards, however, " el amor de la patria venció," and he returned to Valladolid, then the capital of Spain, in 1604.

As Figueroa makes no mention of his father, we infer that at this time he also was dead. " Here," he continues, " in my native country, the paths of any pretension whatever were closely barred, which abroad I had found wide open." It was while in Valladolid, probably in March, 1605, that he got into a quarrel, stabbed his opponent, took refuge in a church and afterward fled in disguise to Baeza, thence to Ubeda, Jaen and Granada. He then went to Seville, of the climate of which he complains, but praises the women of that city, who are " swarthy, graceful, of good disposition, agreeable conversation and attractive be-

Pastor Fido. Tragicomedia pastoral de Battista Guarino. Traducida de Italiano en verso Castellano por Christoval Suarez. Napoles, Tarquinio Longo, 1602. He says: "Los traductores de Ticknor no han podido verla." It is true that the Spanish translators of Ticknor had never seen this edition of 1602, but they had seen an edition of 1622, by Christoval Suarez, "Doctor en ambos derechos," and that on comparing this edition with that of 1609, the difference is at once apparent. The latter is, moreover, addressed to the Duke of Mantua and Montferrato, while the former is dedicated to D. Juan Battista Valenzuela Velazquez. "Authors and book-sellers," they continue, "were not at that time in the habit of changing the dedications of their books without good reasons." Vol. III, p. 543. They believe the edition of 1622 at Naples to be a reprint of that of 1602, and, hence, is not by Suarez de Figueroa. The difference between the translation of 1609, known to be Figueroa's, and that of 1622, is such that it is hardly possible that both were made by the same person. What complicates the matter is that we know that Figueroa was in Naples in 1600-02. One Christoval Suarez Treviño contributed a *Glossa de Burlas* to the poetical tournament held at Madrid in 1620. It has been conjectured that he is the translator of the edition of 1602. See *Justa Poetica,* etc., Madrid, 1620, fol. 117v, and also Crawford, *op. cit.,* p. 23, who discusses the matter in detail.

cause of the suavity of their voices, which makes their pro-
nunciation exceedingly agreeable." From Seville he went
to San Lucar, and finaly to Madrid. Here, he says, " I returned to my early life, to the past painful idleness. I
took up my pen, and for my amusement wrote some
sketches which were kindly received by scholars." " Still,"
he continues, " I could not dismiss from my thoughts the
continual anxiety of absenting myself to seek in strange
lands those who in former times had served me so gener-
ously as a shield and protection." And when asked whether
there was no prince in Spain who might lend him a hand
on account of his studies and experiences, and being told
that the complaint of " los mas ingeniosos," continually oppressed by poverty, was of long standing, he replied: " Es
cosa insufrible profesar, teniendo cortas partes, exquisita
libertad de animo, requisito que por ningun caso adquiere
alicion. Posseo las dos circunstancias que casi sienpre
suelen andar unidas, sovervio y pobre. De mi boca no ha
de salir adulacion."

He speaks with bitterness of the Count of Lemos, the
patron of Cervantes, to whom he dedicated a book and to
whose presence he says that he was not even admitted, and
that he returned from Barcelona to Madrid " without
speaking to or seeing the face of him who had been the
principal object of that journey." Indeed, he says, " you
should know that of the seven books that I have published,
three were dedicated to persons whose faces I have never
seen, though I was at Court." [1]

From this we should infer that Figueroa was out of
favor at Court, and consequently out of office, and this,
indeed, he tells us in 1620,[2] though in the sentence imme-

---

[1] *El Passagero,* fol. 376.

[2] *Varias Noticias,* in the prologue he says: " Asi mientras su Magestad no me empleare en la continuacion de su seruicio," etc.

diately preceding, far from assuming the disgruntled, dissatisfied tone which he here shows, he tells us that his works had been well received and that his country had received him kindly and with no less generosity, enabling him to maintain himself many years " en sitio de tantas obligaciones como la Corte." Besides, in a letter which he wrote in 1624, he states that he had been in the King's service twenty-seven years.[1] However this may be, in 1622, when Don Antonio Alvarez de Toledo, Duke of Alba, became Viceroy of Naples, Figueroa petitioned him for a post in Italy, and on February 22, 1623, he was appointed Auditor of the town of Lecce.[2] Here his conduct in suppressing the lawlessness that then reigned was so vigorous (he hanged five men and sent a hundred to the galleys) that he was dismissed from office on August 8, 1623, and was not thereafter reinstated.

In December, 1627, Figueroa was " Auditor de la Regia Udienza " in Catanzaro, in the province of Calabria.[3] At this time he fell into the hands of the Inquisition for freeing from prison one Francesco Antonio Stantione, an officer of the Viceroy, who had attempted to gather taxes from the ecclesiastical orders and who had been imprisoned by the Bishop of Nicotera in that town.[4] As a result of the

---

[1] Rennert, *Some Documents in the Life of Christoval Suarez de Figueroa,* " Mod. Lang. Notes," 1892. " Veynte y siete años ha que siruo al rey en diferentes cargos con certificaciones de Virreyes de mi buen proceder; con cartas de su Magestad en que lo confiesa y se da por bien seruido, prometiendome en ellas aumentos y honras; solo aqui ve degenerado, perdiendo en un punto lo adquerido en tanto tiempo: suma desgracia " (p. 405).

[2] Crawford, *l. c.,* p. 79.

[3] Rennert, *Some Documents,* etc., p. 410.

[4] *Some Documents,* etc., *Modern Lang. Notes,* Vol. VII, p. 410, and Crawford, *l. c.,* pp. 81 *et seq.,* where the proceedings are given at length.

clash between the Viceroy and the church authorities, Figueroa, on January 25, 1630, was arrested and imprisoned by the officers of the Inquisition,[1] first in Castil Nuovo, where he remained seventeen days, and then in the " Carceri della Nunziatura," where he seems to have been confined until July, 1631.   On January 3, 1633, he was appointed " Abogado fiscal de la Audiencia " at Trani,[2] and on October 10th of that year he signed the " Licencia " of the pastoral romance, *Los Pastores del Betis* of Gonzalo de Saavedra, which was published in that city.   We do not know the date of Figueroa's death; it was after 1644, however, in which year he issued his epic poem *España Defendida,* which appeared at Naples in that year.

It is not difficult, after reading this autobiographical sketch in the *Passagero,* to form an opinion of Figueroa's character.   His must have been a narrow and selfish nature, and the sarcastic and deprecating tone in which, in his *Passagero,* he speaks of Cervantes is ill requiting the kindness of his great contemporary, (over whom the grave had barely closed), for his praise in *Don Quixote,* Part I, chap. lxii, and again, only two years before the latter's death, in the *Journey to Parnassus.*   Indeed Figueroa's unfaithful and ungrateful character is manifest throughout his works.   He speaks well of none of his fellow-writers, but scatters his malevolent words freely among those more favored than himself.[3]   He was a member of that great army of office-seekers in Spain, which first came into prominence in the time of Charles V., and for which recruits have never been wanting down to the present day.   He was of an unloving and unlovable nature,—a disappointed and

[1] *Modern Lang. Notes,* Vol. VII, p. 409.

[2] Crawford, *op. cit.,* p. 86.

[3] See his attack upon Lope de Vega, *Passagero,* fols. 103 and 108.

carping man, at odds with the world, which, doubtless treated him as he deserved.

The *Constante Amarilis* was not very successful, as the author himself says. In the prologue he gives its purpose: " my intention has been to celebrate the constancy and suffering of two persecuted lovers, from the beginning of their lives to their happy marriage." Some time prior to the appearance of the *Constante Amarilis,* Figueroa had entered the service of Don Juan Andrés Hurtado de Mendoza, who was living at Barajas, a town in the province of Cuenca. It was to this friendship that the *Constant Amarilis* owes its origin.[1] In it, Figueroa appears at Damon, and the marriage celebrated in the romance is that of his patron D. Juan Andrés Hurtado de Mendoza (Menandro) with his third wife, who was also his cousin, Doña Maria de Cárdenas (Amarilis), daughter of D. Bernardino de Cárdenas, Duke of Maqueda and of Doña Luisa Manrique de Lara, Duchess of Nájera, on March 29, 1609.

The *Constante Amarilis,* the author tells us, was written in two months. It is composed of four " discourses," and is a dull book, which all the author's poetical talent failed to make interesting. That Figueroa had carefully read and remembered the *Arcadia* of Sannazaro is at once apparent. He has, however, introduced many incidents that are quite foreign to a work of this kind, such as the long discourse of Menandro on the art of poetry, nor are there any descriptions of natural scenery anywhere in the book, which might have been written by a poet who had never ventured beyond the walls of his native city. Appended are a number of the best poems:

[1] Crawford (*op. cit.,* p. 30), who has succeeded in identifying the principal characters in the romance, v. also, *Mod. Lang. Notes,* Vol. XXI (1906), pp. 8-11.

Tercetos.

Mas ay de mi! quien oye mis lamentos?
  ay! que valen si el ayre se los lleva,
  y siempe fueron sin piedad los vientos!

Sueño, si cosa hize que no deva
  contra ti, ya te hallas satisfecho,
  ya es tiempo que a mi bien de mi des **nueva**.

Dile, qu'estoy en lagrimas desecho,
  y huyendo ve sin estorvar mi gloria,
  el daño baste que hasta aqui m'has **hecho**.

Hermano de la muerte, que vitoria
  sacaras deste trance, si embidioso
  usurpas de mis ansias la memoria?

Es la noche al amante desseoso,
  apazible, cortes y lisongera,
  deteniendo su curso presuroso:

Tu assi, vaso y licor d'Adormidera
  con qu'en ocio sepultas los mortales
  cortes arroja de tu mano fiera.

Y vos, queridas puertas, dad señales
  de ser por gusto, y por piedad aora
  el unico remedio de mis males.

Sus alas tiende ya la bella Aurora,
  ya se mueven, ya cantan Ruiseñores,
  puertas, dexadme ver à mi señora:

Qu'a vuestro ser aplicaré loores,
  y colgando guirnaldas amorosas
  vuestro umbral cubriré de varias flores.

*   *   *   *   *   *   *

Levantaos con silencio de la tierra,
  y concededme entrada poco a poco,
  mi bien sereys, sereys paz de mi guerra.

*   *   *   *   *   *   *

Ten lastima de mi (ó Tarsia mia)
  sino oirás en toda noche oscura,
  mis llantos, y mis quexas a porfia.

Vos puertas, vos sereys mi sepoltura
sino mudais la desdichada suerte
de quien en vos à puesto su ventura.

Piedad mostrad, y evitareys mi muerte,
no tengais por dificil qualquier medio,
que si professa ser mi pena fuerte,
fuerte tambien serà vuestro remedio. (pp. 68-71).

Cancion de Meliseo.

* * * * * * *

Centella buelta ya la losa fria,
harán obsequias sobre el cuerpo muerto;
la piedra bañarán con tierno llanto;
llenarán de suspiros el desierto;
y en memoria del Ioven, a porfia
tristes entonarán funebre canto.
Las ninfas entretanto,
offrecerán piadosas
guirnaldas olorosas;
adornarán con ellas los altares;
y en partiendo d'alli se oirán cantares
endechas tristes d'aves diferentes:
si a caso te llegares
leerás las letras que verás presentes.

Huesped, cubre este marmol un lloroso
Amante, de prisiones desatado:
sabras que fue la causa de su muerte
la que fue de su gloria y su cuidado.
Aqui sus huesos gozan del reposo
qu'en vida les negó su triste suerte;
si quieres detenerte
mira la sepoltura
a quien dan sombra oscura
estos laureles, cuyo movimiento
provocan a tristeza al mas contento:
las galas de los arboles despoja
enrronquecido viento,
y secase en cayendo aqui la oja. (p. 101).

Sonnet.

Tendio la noche el tenebroso engaño,
  y difunta dexó l'alma del dia:
  Morfeo en los mortales esparcia
  el qu'es de nuestra vida desengaño:
Quando yo por huir d'ausencia el daño
  de Elisa el dulce albergue recorria:
  su rostro vi, por quien la sombra fria
  de luz y ardor cubrio su negro paño.
Mientras el cielo (dixe) tantos ojos
  abre quantos el suelo agora cierra,
  da fin (Elisa bella) a mis enojos.
Cesse (me respondio) d'amor la guerra,
  y pues te doy el alma por despojos
  concede al cuerpo paz qu'es poca tierra. (p. 263).

ESPINEL ADORNO: " THE REWARD OF CONSTANCY."

Over a decade elapsed before the next pastoral romance, "The Reward of Constancy," by Jacinto de Espinel Adorno, appeared in 1620.[1] The author dedicated his work to Don Diego de Añaya y Mendoça, and begs him to receive it favorably, it being his first work, as an earnest of better service in the future. In the address to the reader, he says: " If perchance the language and invention do not please you, remember that a poor wit (*un corto ingenio*) like mine, can do no better," etc., and further, " one thing I would ask of you, and that is, that you read the entire book." This is asking much of the reader, though it was a less disagreeable task than one would have supposed, judging from the opening paragraph; his book, moreover, is the only source of our scanty knowledge of his life, for it is believed that one or two facts put by the author into the mouth of Arsindo, are to be referred to himself. According to this, the author was born at Manilva [2] and brought up at Munda,[3] in the province of Malaga, which he was

[1] *El Premio de la Constancia, y Pastores de Sierra Bermeia. Por Iacinto de Espinel Adorno. Año 1620. En Madrid, Por la viuda de Alonso Martin.* The Sierra Bermeja is a range of mountains on the confines of the provinces of Malaga and Cadiz, in the Ronda chain; called Vermeja from its reddish soil. I have a second edition of the *Premio de la Constancia* published at Seville in 1894, at the expense of the Marqués de Xeres de los Caballeros.

[2] A town of Spain in the province, and fifty-five miles southwest of Malaga, near the coast.

[3] On fol. 36 he tells us that his parents took him to Munda, where

obliged to leave, having wounded his opponent in a nocturnal brawl, the result of an unfortunate love affair.

"The Reward of Constancy" never reached a second edition until our own day, nor is it known that its author published any other work; his name, however, occurs several times as a contributor to the *justas poeticas* of the time.

The book begins as follows: "Adonde con tan pressuroso passo encaminas el curso violento de mi desdicha, termino fatal del rigor (ô suerte contraria) con que apriessa me amenazas : tormento aparente con que aguijoneas, pecho que si no dessea vivir, es por estar a pique de tantos incendios, que muestran el trance duro en que estoy puesto : infelize daño, terrible pena, fragoso tormento, temeraria fatiga, todos juntos contrarios, no temidos deste desdichado, venid, venid, y dadle fin al cuerpo que entre aquestos riscos, solitarias grutas, y cavernosas peñas, aguarda el triste golpe de la parca rigurosa, para conmigo ingrata, no al alma, etc., etc. This, it must be admitted, is not an auspicious beginning.

In the following passage the beauties of a pastoral life are described:

"Aqui, dixo Felino, engañamos la vida lo mejor que podemos, nunca faltos de gusto, ni agenos de regalo, por ser esta vida la mas amada y mas quieta que todas. Aqui estamos alexados y remontados de los negocios y pretenciones de los que andan hechos camaleones de los poderosos Principes. Aqui estamos ya guardando nuestros ganados,

---

they had relatives, and here he was brought up and sent to school. He studid Latin, "no con cuydado por yrme divertiendo en cosas que si importauan al gusto, danauan al alma." And again in Book II, speaking of the poet Vincente Espinel, who was "the first inventor of *dézimas*," also called *espinelas*, and who was born at Munda, Arsindo says: "long have I known him by reputation, not personally,—aunque he estado yo en su patria muchos dias." See also Gayangos' tr. of Ticknor, *History of Spanish Literature*, Vol. III, p. 543.

ya arando y cultiuando los campos y heredades que fueron
de nuestros mayores, cogiendo y abarcando cada uno menos
aun de lo que puede, estando alegres y contentos con solo
dos bueyes, mas que con grandes tesoros los ricos Mon-
arcas. Aqui no tenemos los sobdesaltos que en los rezios
combates los discipulos de Marte tienen con el zumbido de
las lluvias espesas de balas, reliquias de bombardas y cule-
brinas, parte donde cadaqual encoge sus mienbros aunque
mas el animo se dilate, no dexando de tener algun genero
de temor, cada uno por su incierta suerte. . . . Ya mira-
mos los ganados, y rebaños de toros, y vacas, que andan
dando bramidos, vagando por los campos espaciosos, y
valles amenos abundantes, si de pastos, no avaros de aguas.
. . . Ya otras vezes se nos antoja el recostarnos debaxo
de la sombra de una antigua y acopada enzina, cuyo suelo
vestido de grana, nos sirve de entretenernos con blando
sustento, combidando a dulce sueño. . . . Ya oymos quexarse las aves con sus cantos, emboscadas entre las espessas
ramas destas selvas, respondiendose unas a otras, con particular y acordada armonia," etc. (ed. 1894, p. 9).

The book is pleasant reading, its style generally being
easy and agreeable and its descriptions of natural scenery
often very beautiful. Long and dull stories from Greek
and Roman history are, however, also intermingled, and
the shepherds seldom miss an opportunity to indulge in
moralizing. They grapple with some of the profoundest
problems: as an example, Arsileo, speaking of children,
says that punishment is good for them, whereupon Arsindo
says: " No child has ever died from chastisement, but, on
the other hand, from not being chastised in time great
troubles have followed. There is no greater punishment
in this life than not to be punished."

The poetry scattered through the book is not of a very
high order. Here is a sonnet:

Sale el Sol por las cumbras del Oriente
  Para llenar el mundo de alegria,
  Y en la distancia de tan solo un dia
  Su curso gira, y llega al Occidente:
Sigue la noche luego velozmente,
  Muestra su manto azul de argenteria,
  Diana sale que en su plata fia
  Del cielo al suelo puesta frente a frente:
Sale risueña la rosada Aurora,
  Y la mañana que los campos dora;
  Buelue a llenar los prados de contento
  El Sol con su dichoso navimiento:
  Y todo tiene fin, que es sombra vana
  El Sol, la noche, el Alua, y la mañana (*ibid.*, p. 37).

Song of the Dryads.

Las fuentes que al alua matiza
quando hace al mundo salua,
con gusto alegre risueñas
saltan, bullen, brillan y dançan.
Si el ausentarse la noche
las seluas estan vizarras
con la venida de Cintia,
que las adorna y engasta.
Y las avezillas libres
con harpados picos cantan,
pidiendo albricias al dia
y el fin de sus esperanças.
Y los campos apacibles
con rosicleres de nacar
forman a la vista cielo,
y a los olfatos dan ambar,
Todos con el nueuo huesped,
que ya sus alfombras passa
con gusto alegre, risueños,
saltan, bullen, brillan, y dançan (*ibid.*, p. 240).

Sometimes the author descends to mere word-quibbling, as in the following sonnet, which is sung by Fenicia and Laureno (Book II, fol. 61).

Laur. Temblando miro si constante adoro
    rostro que engendra gloria, triste llanto:

Fen.   Yo siento pena, si contenta canto,
        descubro el mal, y mi remedio ignoro:
Laur. Sufro temor, si aguardo mi tesoro.
Fen.   Lagrimas muestro, si mi bien espanto:
Laur. Tanto me aclaro, que me pierdo tanto,
Fen.   Quanto me anima amor, tanto mas lloro.
Laur. Mi bien espero. *Fen.* Mi contento aguardo.
Laur. Huyo del mal. *Fen.* Pretendo mi ventura.
Laur. Tristezas me da amor. *Fen.* A mí tormento.
Laur. Tarda la dicha. *Fen.* Yo en gozarla tardo.
Laur. Temo. *Fen.* Vazilo. *Laur.* Tiempo. *Fen.* Coyuntura.
Laur. Espera. *Fen.* Aguarda. *Laur.* El pecho. *Fen.* El pensamiento.

" THE SHEPHERD OF CLENARDA " BY BOTELLO.

In 1622 Miguel Botello published in Madrid his pastoral romance " The Shepherd of Clenarda." [1] In another work, *La Filis,* [2] he calls himself Captain Miguel Botello de Carvallo. He was a Portuguese, born at Viseo in 1595; in 1622 (his vessel left Lisbon on March 18th) he accompanied, as secretary, the fourth Count of Vidiguerra, D. Francisco de Gama, when he sailed for India as Viceroy. [3] Having returned to his native country, he went to Paris in 1647, in the retinue of Don Francisco's son, D. Vasco

---

[1] *Prosas y Versos del Pastor de Clenarda, por Miguel Botello, natural de la ciudad de Viseo. Con licencia, en Madrid, por la viuda de Fernando Correa de Montenegro,* MDCXXII. 8°.

[2] *La Filis. Del Capitan Miguel Botello de Carvallo. Al Conde de la Vidiguerra. En Madrid, por Juan Sanchez.* Año 1641. It is a poem in six cantos, written in octaves (Gallardo, *Ensayo,* II, p. 127). Previously he had published *La Fabula de Piramo y Tisbe,* dedicated to two Genoese nobles, D. Francisco and D. Andres Fiesco, Madrid, 1621. He is the author of two other works: *Soliloquios a Christo N. S.* (in verse), Paris, 1645, and *Rimas varias y Tragi-comedia del martir d'Ethiopia,* En Ruan, en la inprenta de Lorenço Maury. Año MDCXLVI. It contains, among others, commendatory verses by Antonio Henriquez Gomez, most of whose works were also published at Rouen. In this work Botello styles himself " Secretario del Exmo. señor Conde Almirante."

[3] " Ao chegar a Moçambique, travou-se peleja com uma frota de hollandezes, ficando Miguel Botelho ferido na testa. Aportou a Gôa a 19 de dezembro. D'aqui foi Miguel Botelho despachado para o sul por capitão de um patacho, com o encargo de levar cartas ao governador de Maninha. De regreso a India encontrou-se com uma nau hollandeza, com a qual se bateu como valoroso soldado. . . . Miguel Botelho achava-se em Hespanha, sem duvida militando na Catalunha quando em Portugal rebentou o movimento revolucionario que proclamou a nossa autonomia. D'aqui não sem graves difficultades e perigos conseguiu elle passar a França," etc. *Archivo Historico Portugues,* Vol. IV (1906), p. 317.

Luis de Gama, first Marquis of Niza, who was sent to that Court as Ambassador extraordinary in that year. As he returned to Portugal on April 30, 1649, it is probable that Botello returned with him.[1] The latest notice we have of Botello is in 1654.[2]

" The Shepherd of Clenarda," a pastoral romance in prose and verse, the chief personages of which are Lisardo and Clenarda, is divided into four books. Prefixed are a number of laudatory versés by Spanish *ingenios,* including Da. Maria de Zayas, Manuel de Faria y Sousa (" to the author, on his leaving for India "), Alonso de Salas Barbadillo, D. Rodrigo de Herrera, " his best friend ", and Antonio Lopez de Vega. The latter addresses the poet as Lisardo, indicating that Botello has represented himself under this disguise. In his *Fabula de Piramo y Tisbe* he tells us that his pastoral romance is a " historia disfrazada, si bien verdadera." I have never seen a copy of this very rare book.[3]

---

[1] See *O primeiro Marquez de Niza,* by José Ramos-Coelho, in *Archivo Historico Portugues,* I, Lisbon, 1903. On August 2, 1647, he writes from Paris: "De Madrid me vem agora todas as obras do grande Lope de Vega; e são quarenta e cinco livros que não tinha " (p. 38). Botello is not mentioned in this article. See also Barrera, *Catálogo,* p. 44.

[2] " Pelos seus longos serviços, tanto em Paris como na India, o agraciou D. João IV., em 1649, com o habito de Christo, dando-lhe em 1654 a pensão de vinte mil reis na commenda de ¡Ranhados, em que estava provido D. Fernão Manuel. *Archivo Historico Portugues,* IV, p. 317.

[3] Gallardo (*Ensayo,* II, p. 126) says of it: " La prosa y los versos son faciles y corrientes, pero no tienen colores ni conceptos señalados que distingan á Botello privilegiadamente entre los ingenios de su tiempo. Su estilo es más florero que florido. El corriente de su prosa se parece á la del Dr. Lozano, aunque la de este es más rica." See also Garcia Peres, *Catálogo razonado de los Autores portugueses que escribieron en Castellano.* Madrid, 1890, p. 58. Botello also contributed verses to the *Justa poetica* in honor of San Isidro, held at Madrid in 1620. See Gallardo, *Ensayo,* IV, p. 973.

CUEVAS: "THE EXPERIENCES OF LOVE AND FORTUNE."

FOUR years afterward, in 1626, Francisco de Quintana, a friend of Lope de Vega, under the name of Francisco de las Cuevas, published " The Experiences of Love and Fortune." [1] Quintana was born in Madrid, and in 1626 became a member of the Congregation of Saint Peter, in which he served the cause of the church with great zeal, and seems to have had considerable reputation for eloquence as a preacher. In 1644 he became rector of the

---

[1] *Experiencias de Amor y Fortuna. A Lope Felix de Vega Carpio, Procurador Fiscal de la Camara Apostolica, y su Notario descrito en el Archiuo Romano, Familiar del Santo Oficio de la Inquisicion. Por el Licenciado Francisco de las Cuevas, natvral de Madrid. Año (In oblectatione saepe est doctrina) 1626. Con Privilegio. En Madrid,* Por la Vivda de Alonso Martin. Salvá (no. 1780) describes an edition "Madrid, Francisco Martinez, 1632, 8°, 16 + 276 fols., and I have a note of one: Montilla, Francisco Martinez, 8°, 6 + 258 fols. The next ed. (which I possess), is Barcelona, por Pedro Lacavalleria, 1633, 8°, 8 + 156 fols. There were also editions of Madrid, 1641; Jaen, 1646; Barcelona, 1649; Madrid, 1666 and 1723. That the *Experiencias* passed through so many editions is evidence that it enjoyed considerable popularity, and shows how easily the public taste was satisfied. The book is no better and no worse, however, than the author's next attempt, the *Historia de Hipolito y Aminta,* first published in Madrid in 1627. It is written in the manner of the *Persiles y Sigismunda* of Cervantes, and was perhaps prompted by it. Quintana's literary success was doubtless due, in no small measure, to the powerful influence of his friend, Lope de Vega. It may be mentioned that an English translation of " The Experiences of Love and Fortune" appeared in 1651. It is entitled: *The History of Don Fenise. A new Romance, written in Spanish by Francisco de las Coveras (sic). And now Englished by a person of honour.* 8°. London. Printed by Humphrey Moseley, 1651.

188

Hospital de la Latina in Madrid. Such, however, were the litigations and entanglements in which Quintana became involved, that he was reduced to the greatest poverty. He died January 25, 1658.[1]

" The Experiences of Love and Fortune " is dedicated to Quintana's friend, Lope de Vega, who, in an address prefixed to the work, speaks of it as " esta primera piedra de sus estudios, aunque tan sazonado fruto de sus verdes años." From this it is evident that Cuevas, as we may now call him, was then a young man, and this may be some excuse for his very commonplace book. It is divided into five *poemas,* " because *poema* is a generic name which embraces not only verses, but also prose, as Cicero intimates in his book *De Oratore,"* etc. He concludes thus: " I do not think that the learned will be displeased with reading it, for as Quintilian says: ' *In grandibus coenis hoc saepe nobis accidit, ut cum optimis saciati sumus, varietas tamen nobis ex vilioribus grata sit.' "*

The first " poem " begins thus:

" No lexos de una pequeña fuente, que a un verde sauze puso de transparente cristal candidas prisiones, Siluio, pastor por su entendimiento, y por su disposicion celebrado en los montes que a la Imperial Toledo vezinos, son aspera poblacion de duros robles, o albergue poco culto, a varias fieras, mayoral de un mediano aprisco, dueño de un apacible rebaño, que a trechos era esmalte del prado, nieue del monte, siendo en partes aumentado de las peñas; estaua una tarde, de las que suauamente alienta Mayo, respirando a un tiempo zefiros y flores, tan melancolico, que ni los campos le diuertian, ni las fuentes le dauan alegria; antes le sucedia tan al contrario (efeto antiguo de los perfetos

---

[1] Alvarez y Baena, *Hijos de Madrid,* Vol. II, p. 152; Barrera, *Biografía de Lope de Vega,* in *Obras de Lope de Vega,* I, Madrid, 1890, p. 502.

tristes) que le seruia de mortal veneno lo que pudiera sanar sus fieros males."

Here is a passage from the second " poem " :

" La malicia de los presentes siglos, tan conforme en todo a la de los passados, nos muestra claramente, que siempre ha sido uno mismo el mundo, y siempre flaca nuestra naturaleza. Quando yo miro que Seneca in Agam. dize estas palabras: Perecieron las costumbres, la fuerça, la piedad, y la verguença, que una vez perdida, ignora los caminos de boluer a su dueño; pienso, o que Feniso viuio en tiempo de Seneca, o que Seneca estuuo presente a los sucessos de Feniso. Sano de su indisposicion estaua, solicito restaurar su perdida pretendia, y cuerdo su sentimiento ocultaua nuestro noble Cauallero a tiempo que una mañana de las que el hermoso padre del dia calienta las duras escamas de Escorpion, llegó cansado de hazer ocultas diligencias a su posada y casa de Leonardo, no halló en ella a don Luis, porque le desuelaua el mismo cuydado; y assi opresso de su imaginacion (tormento que mata sin acabar la vida, y daño, cuyo remedio es tan dificultoso, como contra enemigo inescusable) se arrojó sobre la cama para descansar, porque viue engañado el que piensa que los pesares no cansan el cuerpo, quando atormentan el alma."

As a specimen of the verse in " The Experiences of Love and Fortune," I have copied the following *Epigrama,* which the shepherds sing upon seeing Theodora with a carnation (clavel) in her mouth.

> Clauel hermoso que espirando olores
>   Al dulce aliento de mi bien te mueues,
>   No se inquietan tus hojas por ser leues,
>   Antes son de temor essos temblores.
> Al competirte injurias otras flores,
>   Y es bien igual rigor aora prueues,
>   Aunque á tu osada competencia deues
>   El tener de verguença essas colores.

Pienso que fueran tus consejos sabios
  Si mudáras el ser, si cristal fueras,
  Iuzgarante reflexos de sus labios;
  Mas en tanta porfia es bien que infieras,
Que por necio mereces mas agrauios,
Pues viendote exceder, vencer esperas (fol. 44).

Here are some *decimas:*

No sé si se llame amor
  á esto que mi pecho alcança,
  que amor y sin esperança
  mas me parece rigor:
  el impossible mayor
  no consiste en ser mi empleo
  indigno deste trofeo,
  porque el mayor impossible
  aduierto en no ser possible
  todo quanto yo deseo.
Vuestra beldad me assegura
  de que con razon me empeño,
  de mi pecho os haze dueño
  deseos de mi ventura:
  vuestro ingenio me procura
  quitar vida y libertad,
  mas en la seguridad
  con que mis afectos nacen,
  deshaze el temor quanto hazen
  deseo, ingenio, y beldad (fol. 103).

The book, to the credit of its author, contains very little verse. It is written in the bad taste of much of the prose of the time, with a piling-up of epithets and constant resort to antithetical clauses. "The Experiences of Love and Fortune," should, however, be expunged from the list of pastoral romances in which it has so long figured, for it is a romance of adventure simply, made up of most improbable incidents, the second "poem" containing an episode based upon the old story of *Ami et Amile*.

CORRAL: " THE CYNTHIA OF ARANJUEZ."

THREE years had elapsed when, in 1629, *La Cintia de
Aranjuez,* by Don Gabriel de Corral, appeared at Madrid.[1]
The author, who was the son of Garcia de Corral and
Ysabel de Villalpando, was born at Valladolid, where he
was baptized on March 31, 1588.[2] He became chaplain to
the Constable of Castile, and three years before the ap-
pearance of the " Cinthia " he had published a translation
of the " Argenis " of Jean Barclay, entitled: *La Prodigiosa
Historia de los dos Amantes, Argenis y Poliarco,* Madrid,
Juan Gonzalez, 1626, 4°.[3] He also translated from the
Latin the poetical works of Pope Urban VIII.

The earliest appearance of Corral as an author, to my

[1] *La Cintia de Aranivez, Prosas y Versos. Por el Licenciado Don
Gabriel de Corral, natural de Valladolid. Al Excelentissimo Señor
Condestable de Castilla, mi señor.* [Arms of the Constable.] *En
Madrid. En la Imprenta del Reyno. A costa de Alonso Perez, Lib-
rero de su Magestad.* Año MDCXXIX. 8°, viii + 208 ff. I possess
a copy.

[2] Partida de bautismo: " Grabiel = En treinte y uno de março de
1588 años baptice a gabriel hijo de Garcia de corral y de ysabel de
billalpando su muger fueron padrinos Antonio bauptista de çamora
y maria alonso Abogado S. Andres." Cortés, *Una Corte literaria,* p.
167; and the same author's article on Gabriel de Corral in the *Revista
Contemporanea* (Enero, 1903), which I was unable to consult. Sr.
Cortes says: " Tuvo Gabriel un hermano, Juan, bautizado en la Antigua, y una hermana Casilda, bautizada en S. Martin." After this
account was finished I had the pleasure of receiving a copy of Sr.
Cortés' article in the *Revista,* for which I wish to thank him most
cordially. I have made some additions from his article.

[3] The *Argenis* of Barclay, written in Latin, was first printed in
1621. A French translation appeared as early as 1623.

knowledge, is found in some Latin distichs which he wrote to Montalvan's *Orfeo* in 1624.[1] He also wrote a laudatory *decima* to Castillo Solorzano's *Tardes entretenidas,* 1625. In 1631 he is mentioned among the distinguished poets of the time by Sebastian Francisco de Medrano,[2] and seems to have enjoyed considerable reputation as a writer of verse.

In the prologue to the " Cynthia," dated Zaragoça, August 15, 1628, Corral says that he is writing these " sketches " on his journey to Rome, without books or help (*prevencion*) of any kind, " no para estimacion, sino para dar a entender mi afecto asi a la pluma, como a la atencion de los obligaciones que V. Merced me ha puesto," etc. Our author passed some years in Italy, being at Rome in 1632 in the service of the Count of Monte-Rey, the

[1] Unless, as is very probable, our author is the same person as El Licenciado Gabriel Garcia de Corral, who contributed verses to the *certamen poetico* published by Pedro de Herrera in his *Descripcion de la Capilla de nuestra Señora del Sagrario,* etc., Madrid, 1617. Salvá, *Catálogo,* No. 260. I am glad to learn that Sr. Cortés is also of the opinion that they are one person.

[2] In his *Favores de las Musas,* Milan, 1631. See Gallardo, *Ensayo,* Vol. III, col. 702. Some unedited poems by Corral are found in a MS. in the Biblioteca Nacional, Madrid (M. 202). *Ibid.,* Vol. II, Appendix, p. 35. According to D. Luis Fernandez-Guerra y Orbe, *Alarcon,* p. 336, Corral belonged to the famous *Academia poética* in Madrid, in 1622, of which all the most celebrated poets were members, including Lope de Vega, Mira de Mescua, Guillen de Castro, Luis Vélez de Guevara, Alarcon, and others. Hartzenbusch, in his preliminary study of Alarcon's works (*Comedias de D. Juan Ruiz de Alarcon y Mendoza,* p. xxxiv, in Bibl. de Autores Españoles), had already called attention to the *vejamen dado en una academia* in which all who entered into the *concurso* were greatly caricatured, and among whom Corral also figures. The account is interesting, but is too long to be copied here. I do not find any notice of this particular *vexamen* in the *Obras de Anastasio Pantaleon de Ribera,* Madrid, 1634, which I have. In the *vexamen segundo* (*ibid.,* fol. 143v) he figures as " el Licenciado Coriandro."

Spanish Ambassador.[1] Returniing to Spain, he was made Canon of Zamora, and afterwards Superior of the Collegial Church at Toro, which office he certainly held in 1640,[2] and apparently until his death, which took place in Toro in November, 1646.[3]

Barrera is of the opinion that two authors of the same name, Gabriel de Corral, existed in Spain at the beginning of the seventeenth century.[4] The grounds, however, for such an opinion are very slight, presumably because a play has come down to us, *La Trompeta del Juizio,* by Gabriel de Corral, printed in Vol. XXXI of the *Comedias nuevas escogidas de los mejores Ingenios de España,* Madrid, 1669.

[1] In this year Montalban wrote of him: "D. Gabriel del Corral, que oy está en Roma en seruicio del Conde de Monterrey, las [comedias] escriuió como quien quiere prouar la pluma en lo menos, excelentissimamente." "Memoria de los que escriuen Comedias en Castilla solamente," in *Para Todos,* ed. of 1645, fol, 278v. That Corral was in Italy prior to 1630, is also shown by Lope de Vega's *Laurel de Apolo,* Silva III; see also Silva VIII, in which Lope calls him the Spanish Propertius.

[2] In the *Obras de Don Luis de Ulloa Pereira,* first published in 1659, there is an "Epistola de D. Gabriel de Corral, Abad entonces de la Iglesia Colegial de Toro." In my copy, which is of the second edition, Madrid, 1674, it occurs on pp. 155-160, and is dated February 26, 1640. This *epistola* is also printed in Böhl v. Faber's *Floresta,* Vol. III, p. 365, No. 981. Barrera says of Corral: "D. Francisco de Vitoria, D. Gabriel del Corral, D. Luis de Ulloa Pereira y sus hijos, en algunas temporadas, y tal cual otro ingenio, formaban en Toro una tertulia, que probablemente se reuniria y haria la corte (por los años de 1643 al de 1645) en el palacio del destronado ministro," i. e. the Count Duke of Olivares. *Catálogo,* p. 499; see also *Nueva Biografía de Lope de Vega,* p. 403.

[3] Partida de difuncion: "Don Gabriel de Corral, Abad que fué de esta Santa Iglesia, se enterró en ella en veinta y siete de Noviembre dicho año de 1646; hizo testamento ante Alonso Rodriguez Dávila, Scriv° de esta ciudad de Toro; testamentarios Don Juo. Brabo, idem, Antonio de la Sierra, Abad que al presente es." Cortés, in *Revista Contemporánea,* 1903, p. 17.

[4] *Catálogo,* p. 101.

There can scarcely be a doubt that the Gabriel García de Corral mentioned in a previous note and our author are one and the same person; no more than it can be doubted that Lope de Vega in the two passages of his *Laurel de Apolo* refers to but one poet. Besides we have the direct testimony of Montalvan that our author was well known as a dramatist before 1632.[1]

Unlike Lope de Vega, in the prologue to his *Arcadia*, Corral tells us in his address to the reader, that he does not write for the cultivated, saying: "No hablo con los Patricios de la cultura, sino con el vulgo[2] con quien Marcial se entiende tal vez diziendo, *Vobis pagina nostra dedicatur*," and again: "I, at least, desire to please the people." He tells us how the book was made up: "I shall confess to you that all the verses this volume contains were written *antes del intento;* and in order to make them acceptable, I have linked them with prose and accompanied them with these discourses, not daring to publish the mere *rimas,* in doing which, men of greater intellect run a risk that is well known. . . . What seemed more venturesome, was to pub-

---

[1] For an account of *La Trompeta del Juizio*, see the articles of Cortés, already mentioned. There is a MS. (xvii century) of *La gran Comedia de la Trompeta del Juicio,* proceeding from the Osuna collection, in which it is ascribed to D. Francisco de Rojas on the title-page, though the concluding lines of the play declare it to be the work of two poets. Sr. Cotarelo says: "Esto será lo más cierto: Corral y Rojas habrán compuesto la comedia, y sólo allá muchos años después de muertos ambos, el editor se la habrá adjudicado al que sería autor del acto primero ó de la primera mitad de la Obra." *Francisco de Rojas Zorrilla,* Madrid, 1911, p. 259.

[2] Concerning this expression, Wolf says: "Dass daruntur noch immer nicht der Pöbel, ja dass unter diesem Spanischen *Vulgo* noch ein sehr achtbarer Theil der Nation, die ganze ländliche und kleinstädtische Bevölkerung im Gegensatz zu den Hauptstädten auch damals (mitte des 16 Jahrhunderts) noch begriffen gewesen sei,—hat Huber (*Gött. Anz.,* 1857, s. 452) sehr gut nachgewiesen. *Studien zur Gesch. d. Spanischen u. Port. Nationalliteratur,* p. 543, n.

lish a book for diversion or entertainment, although pure and exemplary, when, from the nature of my studies, more serious matters were expected." The author succeeded in making a prosy and tiresome book, which is quite a task to read.

It is very probable that some real personage is concealed under the name Cynthia. On fol. 16, there is an allusion to " un Heroe de los mas insignes que tuuo el tronco de los Guzmanes, de quien Cintia era hermosa rama "; on fol. 68 we read: " El soneto fue de Liseno. Celebró anticipado en vaticinio al heroe generoso don Gaspar de Guzman." Again on fol. 95: " Este (dixo) señalando un bizarro varon, es padre de mi señora Cintia, cauallero que por su valor y sangre tuuo grandes puestos." Cintia takes lessons in Latin (fol. 115); she lived in Guadalajara (fol. 123v), and Lisardo, who is in love with her, turns out to be her half-brother (*ibid.*). Cynthia's relatives brought her to Madrid (fol. 124); here she was betrothed against her will, and as a relief from " her illness and melancholy," she retires to the solitude of this *fingido Arcadia* (fol. 124v). On fol. 189v we are told that Cynthia is " doña Guiomar, que ilustra el apellido de los Heroes Guzmanes."

The following " eclogue " which the shepherds sing to a lovely " auditorio de zagales acompañadas de garçones bizarros," will give an idea of the poetry:

> " Dulce remora del viento,
>   Coro entero en una voz,
>   Que fue mordaza inuisible
>   De arroyo murmurador.
> Iman del risco, y del eco,
>   Impossible imitacion,
>   Y de un aliso pomposo
>   Alada y parlera flor.
> Auecilla en fin quexosa
>   De amor, si bien desmintio

A las quexas el concento,
Y la musica al dolor.
  Calla tu cuidado,
  No le digas no,
  Que diran, si le cantas,
  Que te falta amor.
Como blasonas martirios,
  Si en los indicios del Sol
  Madrugan tus sentimientos
  A templarse con tu voz?
Qual amante sus querellas
  Tan suaues disfrazó,
  Si el merito del amar
  Se pierde en la explicacion?
Merezcate amor silencio,
  Imitemonos los dos,
  Aprende a morir callando,
Agradecido al dolor.
  Calla tu cuidado," etc.

Corral is not more fortunate in his sonnets than in his
"eclogues."

Sonnet.

Esta tremula lumbre, que del viento
  Viue sobresaltada y mal segura,
  Atalaya del tiempo, que apresura
  De las horas el facil mouimiento:
Este, o Lelio, alumbrado aduertimiento,
  Que generoso luce lo que dura,
  Que ignorante de noche de hora escura
  La vida ha vinculado al lucimiento:
Indice claro, auiso es eloquente,
  Si de otro que la vista necessitas,
  Y del estudio noble de tu idea,
Para que pues del ayre estas pendiente,
  No a tan breue periodo permitas,
  Accion que de la luz indigna sea (fol. 94b).

The subject of this sonnet (incomprehensible to me) is
a bronze clock: " Laurencio, que no era pobre, en los ador-
nos y galas de su quarto tenia otro relox de bronze, que

libraua su valor eη el artificio, porque con el mayor que hasta entonces se auia visto, el indice de las horas era una luz que las iba alumbrando y señalando."

Book II contains a *vexamen* in which one of the characters expresses astonishment that "there should be hospitals for so many bodies and nations and yet one for poets should be wanting, although they have so many ills." The book is, accordingly, divided into seven *Camas* or beds. We are told, moreover, that "*ha llegado la necessidad poetica a tal estado, que de hambre mas que de intencion, si no se comen, se muerden unos a otros.* No es trato la poesia que ha dado hasta hoy principio a algun mayorazgo, porque los romances y sonetos, aunque sean del Señor Danteo, un año con otro, no valen nada: solo para esta nueua fundacion faltará Medico, ya porque juzgauan la cura destos enfermos impossible, ya porque auia pocas esperanças del stipendio," etc.

Apollo now visits the different beds where the poets lie. The first one he declares "por hetico y tisico; y era asi, porque se auia *desainado de consonantes, y padecia fluxo de sonetos, y colica de romnaces,* a cuyos achaques socorrió con esta receta:

> "Para que por buen camino
>   Engorde este cecinado,
>   Esqueleto amortajado
>   En pieles de pergamino:
> Recipe una gauioneta
>   Tan cortés y comedida,
>   Que le quiera, y no le pida,
>   *Y abstengase de poeta*" (fol. 82).

Lope's high praise of Corral in his *Laurel de Apolo* is another proof, if any were needed of the untrustworthiness of this poem as a help to forming any opinion of Lope's contemporaries.

SAAVEDRA: "THE SHEPHERDS OF THE BÉTIS."

" The Shepherds of the Bétis," [1] by Don Gonzalo de Saavedra,[2] a *Veintequatro* [3] of the city of Cordova, next appeared at Trani, a town of Naples, in 1633. The work was published after the author's death by his son, who dedicated it to Don Manual de Fonseca y Zuñiga, Captain General of the Kingdom of Naples, and calls it " the diversions of my father's youth (*divertimientos de la mocedad de mi padre*). Of its style the son speaks as follows: " The prose is written without verbosity, ingeniously and elegantly; not too profusely nor laconically from affectation; nor is it obscure or prolix, but with well-disposed periods, and with clauses marvelously and helpfully arranged." The following excerpt, which is a very fair example of the style of " The Shepherds of the Bétis," will enable one to form an independent opinion upon this point:

" Entre otras tan famosas, como fertiles, y levantadas sierras, que nuestra Hispano Reyno posee, y lo atraviesen, está una, adonde vienen a juntar los extremos quatro Provincias del, a la qual llaman Sierra de Segura; no sé yo porque, pues no ai persona que lo esté de las hermosas Pas-

---

[1] Bétis, i. e. Guadalquivir.

[2] *Los Pastores del Bétis; Versos y Prosas de Don Gonzalo de Saavedra, veintequatro de la ciudad de Cordoba: dadas a luz por D. Martin de Saavedra y Guzman su hijo, con algunos fragmentos suyos añadidos. Al Ilmo. y Excmo. Sr. D. Manuel de Fonseca y Zuñiga, Conde de Monterey,* etc. En Trani, por Lorenzo Valerij. Año 1633. The license is signed by D. Cristoval Suarez de Figueroa, at Trani, October 10, 1633. See Gallardo, *Ensayo,* IV, p. 296.

[3] *Veintequatro.* The corporation of Seville and other towns in Andalucia, consisted of twenty-four members, called *Veintequatros.*

toras que lo habitan: de la qual un leuantado monte, a quien la naturaleza abrió sus peñascosas entrañas, lança tanta cantidad de agua, que da principio, y nombre a la corriente del celebrado *Bétis,* cuyos poblados margenes de aldeas son causa de que lo esten ellos, y sus hermosos campos de ganados, y perdidos Pastores, de Zagales, que mas cuidosos de amorosos pensamientos, que del gouierno de ellos, oluidados de todo lo que no es mostrar la firmeza de sus voluntades, passaron el tiempo en amorosas juntas. Aqui la maestra naturaleza, usando de su politica inuencion, enriqueció estos Valles de agradables fuentes, contrapuestas a los temporales, assi, que en el ardiente estio apenas las manos pueden resistir la frialdad de sus cristales, y en el riguroso inuierno, en ellos entrados se estienden, y regalan con su templança los encogidos neruios: de algunas de las quales las sobras forman agradables, y murmurantes corrientes, que de amorosos pechos con tiernas lagrimas, aumentadas, llegan fertilizando el distrito, que desde su nacimiento, hasta el famoso rio; inclinando a trechos con su continuo curso, los delgados, y verdes junquillos, y las pintadas y tiernas florecillas, que puestas por limite de su anchura, hermosean sus humedos margenes."

Of Saavedra's poetry, I copy the song of Beliso (p. 79):

> Dulce y sabrosa fuente,
> Si tu cristal enturbian los despojos,
> Y continua corriente
> Que el corazon te ofrece por los ojos,
> Para que te acompañen
> Y destos olmos las raizes bañen.
>
> Porque, como murmuras
> Entre las pedrezuelas, y la arena,
> Remedio no procuras
> Para que cesse mi tormento y pena,
> Y acabados mis males,
> No enturbiara mi llanto tus cristales?

Mueue tu muda lengua
Para reparo de mi triste vida,
Pues mi dolor no mengua,
Ni el rigor de una fiera enpedernida,
Y di a esta ingrata bella
Con la razon que l'alma se querella.

Y tu esmaltado prado
Mas que la misma habitacion de flora,
Si por estar pisado
De los diuinos pies de mi Señora,
A Chipre te auentajas,
Porque mi daño, y su rigor no atajas?

Vosotros airecillos
Que mil vozes formais, dando en las ojas
De aquestos arbolillos,
Formad alguna que de mis congojas
Dé euenta a mi Pastora,
Bella en el rostro, en condicion traidora.

Mas, ay prado florido,
Arboles, aires, fuente dulce y bella,
Que me tiene rendido,
Y ella lo sabe bien, que a no ver ella
Tan rendido mi pecho,
Menos lagrimas fueran de prouecho.

The shepherds are, as is customary, led to the Temple of Diana, and upon one of its columns read the following prophecy:

El que llegare a ver de aquesta casa
Los trasparentes muros de diamante,
O sea pastor libre, o tierno amante
De los que premia Amor con mano escasa,
En llegando a mirar la primer vasa,
Pierda la vista luego en esse instante,
Y dé cuenta sin ella a Dios tonante
De la passion que el corazon le abrasa.
Porque no puede serla manifiesta
A nadie deste templo la grandeza,
Y las cosas que en el hay encerradas,
Hasta que de un Pastor con risa, y fiesta,
De su pastora, mansa la fiereza,
Se celebren las bodas deseadas.

Of this prophecy the sage says:

" Do not trouble yourself to solve it, for it will be in vain, as I assure you that, until the day come in which the Gods permit that this may be fulfilled, it will be impossible for any human intellect however clever (*aventajado*), to understand the mysterious secret hidden in these few letters." " The Shepherds of the Bétis " never reached a second edition.

THE DECLINE OF THE PASTORAL ROMANCES.

THE principal pastoral romances that appeared in Spain for nearly a century after the publication of the *Diana* of Montemayor, have now been passed briefly in review. They all possess the same general characteristics and followed closely in the steps of their Spanish model, though none ever attained the excellence reached by Montemayor. They all picture that ideal life in Arcadia, where the shepherds and shepherdesses " fleet the time carelessly as they did in the Golden World." In none of them is there any attempt at plot or connected narrative; the characters appear and disappear at the will of the author, and nothing was deemed improbable in the forests and meads of their fancied world.

But, while the pastoral romance was finding such great favor in gentler circles, forms of literature had been gradually developing which soon became its formidable rivals; and finally succeeded in obscuring it entirely;—forms of literature that were destined to endure, because they were based upon the national life. In 1554 the " Novela Picaresca " made its appearance in *Lazarillo de Tormes,* and, finally, the national Drama, the foundation of which had been laid as far back as the close of the fifteenth century, was developed with an ardor and enthusiasm for which we find a parallel only in the Greek and English dramatists.

Dramatic literature was popular, because it was written for the whole people. It was hardly considered a respectable form of literature at first, just as we know was the case in England; but it had struck its roots deep in the very heart of Spanish life; it was the faithful mirror of the

Spanish character in all its ages and phases, and finally overshadowed every other form of literary composition. With the advent of the realistic novel and the drama, as illustrators of the national life, the more artificial and courtly pastoral romance gradually disappeared from the scene, but not without leaving its impress upon the literature of Spain. Like the romance of chivalry, it was an important factor in the development of style in Spanish prose, and the easy and graceful diction of Cervantes is doubtless due, in no small measure, to the influence of the pastoral romance, which made itself felt even in the drama; witness the exquisite pictures of rural life which occur in so many of the plays of Lope de Vega.

But the pastoral romance has passed away forever, with the times and the manners that produced it. The singing and sighing of shepherds, that were a pastime and a pleasure in a more ingenuous age, find no responsive echo in this more practical century. And though the *Diana* of Montemayor has been reprinted in our own day, it can hardly be hoped that the fragrance of the fields and forests of its Arcadia is still as perceptible or as agreeable to the modern reader as it was to the reader of three hundred years ago; but considered as a mirror reflecting other times and other conditions, the pastoral romance will always maintain an important place in the literature of the Golden Age of Spain.

APPENDIX.

This *carta* or letter of Montemayor is not to be found in any of his works, so far as I know. That portion of it which relates to his life is here subjoined, copied from the excellent edition of the *Poesias de Francisco de Sâ de Miranda* by Caroline Michaëlis de Vasconcellos. Halle, 1885, p. 655. See p. 20, note 1.

Riberas me erié del rio Mondego,   70
Ado jamas sembró el fiero Marte
Del Rei Marsilio aca desasosiego.
   De ciencia alli alcanzé mui poca parte
I por sola esta parte juzgo el todo
De mi ciencia i estilo, ingenio i arte.   75
   En musica gasté mi tiempo todo;
Previno Dios en mi por esta via
Para me sustentar por algun modo.
   No se fió, señor, de la poesia,
Porque vió poca en mi, i aunque mas viera,   80
Vió ser pasado el tiempo en que valia.
   El rio de Mondego i su ribera
Con otros mis iguales paseava,
Sujeto al crudo amor i su bandera.
   Con ellos el cantar exercitava   85
I bien sabe el amor que mi Marfida
Ia entonces sin la ver me lastimava.
   Aquella tierra fue de mí querida;
Dejé la, aunque no quise, porque veía
Llegado el tiempo ia de buscar vida.   90
   Para la gran Hesperia fue la via
Ado me encaminava mi ventura
I ado senti que amor hiere i porfia.
   Alli me mostró amor una figura;
Con la flecha apuntando dijo : aquella!   95
I luego me tiró con fuerza dura.
   A mi Marfida vi mas i mas bella

Que quantas nos mostró naturaleza,
Pues todo lo de todas puso en ella.

El *mar* de perfecion i gentileza, 100
Fida por la mas fiel que nadie vido,
Suma lealtad de fe i de firmeza.

Mas ia que el crudo amor me huvo herido,
Le vi quedar tan preso en sus amores
Que io fui vencedor siendo vencido. 105

Alli senti de amor tales dolores
Que hasta los de aora no creía
Que los pudiera dar amor maiores.

Pero despues que un mal en mi porfia,
El qual se llama ausencia, es quasi nada 110
El otro grave mal que antes sufria.

En este medio tiempo la estremada
De nuestra Lusitania gran princeza
En quien la fama siempre está ocupada,

Tuvo, señor, por bien de mi rudeza 115
Servir se, un bajo ser alevantado
Con su saber estraño i su grandeza,

En cuia casa estoi ora, pasando
Con mi cansada musa ora en esto,
Ora de amor i ausencia estoi quejando, 120

Ora mi mal al mundo manifiesto;
Ora ordeno partirme, ora me quedo;
En una ora mil vezes mudo el puesto;

Ora, a hurto de amor, me finjo ledo;
Ora me veo tan triste que me muero; 125
Ora querria morir me i nunca puedo.

Mil vezes me pregunto que me quiero
I no sé responder me ni sentir me;
Enfin me hallo tal que desespero. etc.